AVOIDING CYBERFRAUD IN SMALL BUSINESSES

Titles of Related Interest

Accountant's Guide to Fraud Discovery and Control, Second Edition, by Howard R. Davia, Patrick C. Coggins, John C. Wideman, and Joseph T. Kastantin

Accountant's Guide to the Internet, Second Edition, by Eric Cohen

Auditing Information Systems: A Comprehensive Reference Guide, by Jack J. Champlain

Brink's Modern Internal Auditing, Fifth Edition, by Robert Moeller and Herbert N. Witt

Fraud Auditing and Forensic Accounting, Second Edition, by G. Jack Bologna and Robert J. Lindquist

Fraud 101: Techniques and Strategies for Detection, by Howard R. Davia

Montgomery's Auditing, Twelfth Edition, by Vincent M. O'Reilly, Barry N. Winograd, James S. Gerson, and Henry R. Jaenicke

Operational Review: Maximum Results at Efficient Costs, Second Edition, by Rob Reider

For more information on these titles and other Wiley accounting titles, log onto

www.wiley.com/accounting.

AVOIDING CYBERFRAUD IN SMALL BUSINESSES

WHAT AUDITORS AND OWNERS NEED TO KNOW

G. Jack Bologna

Paul Shaw

John Wiley & Sons, Inc.

New York • Chichester • Weinheim • Brisbane • Singapore • Toronto

This publication is designed to provide accurate and authoritative information in regard to the subject matter covered. It is sold with the understanding that the publisher is not engaged in rendering legal, accounting, or other professional services. If legal advice or other expert assistance is required, the services of a competent professional person should be sought.

Library of Congress Cataloging-in-Publication Data:

Bologna, Jack.
    Avoiding cyberfraud in small businesses : what auditors and owners need to know / G. Jack Bologna, Paul Shaw.
        p.   cm.
    Includes index.
    ISBN 0-471-37297-8 (cloth : alk. paper)
    1. Computer crimes.   2. Computer crimes —Prevention.
3. Small business.   4. Commercial crimes.   5. Auditing, Internal.
I. Shaw, Paul (Paul D.)   II. Title.
HV6773.B65   2000
658.4'78— dc21   99-089705

Printed in the United States of America.

10 9 8 7 6 5 4 3 2 1

This book is dedicated to Joseph T. Wells,
a new breed of fraud examiner, whose special talents
in financial investigation and forensic accounting
set him apart from traditional auditors.
His contributions in his field of study also set him
apart from the common practitioner.

Among his many contributions is the creation of the
Association of Certified Fraud Examiners.
Its membership now numbers over 20,000 worldwide.
We owe Joe more than we can ever repay.

To you Joe Wells, thanks for the memories.

—Jack Bologna

ABOUT THE AUTHORS

Jack Bologna is associate professor of management at Siena Heights College in Adrian, Michigan, and the publisher of the monthly newsletters *Forensic Accounting Review* and *Computer Security Digest*. For some 40 years, he has specialized in auditing, investigating, and teaching about white-collar crime, particularly corporate crimes like accounting system frauds and embezzlement. He holds degrees in law and accounting and spent 14 years in federal investigative agencies, including the IRS Intelligence Division and the Drug Enforcement Administration. He has authored and co-authored a number of books on the subjects of law and accounting, including *Accountant's Handbook on Fraud and Commercial Crime*, John Wiley & Sons, New York City, 1992; *Corporate Fraud: The Basics of Prevention and Detection*, Butterworth, Boston, 1983; *Forensic Accounting Handbook, 2nd edition*, Assets Protection Publishing, Madison, WI, 1993; *Fraud Auditing and Forensic Accounting*, John Wiley & Sons, New York City, 1987; *Fraud Awareness Manual*, Assets Protection Publishing, Madison, WI, 1993; and *Corporate Crime Investigation*, Butterworth-Heinemann, Boston, 1997.

Paul Shaw is editor and publisher of *Computing & Communications: Law and Protection* and *Assets Protection*, the latter periodical covering controls and safeguards to protect company resources. He is the co-author of *Fraud Awareness Manual*, Assets Protection Publishing, Madison, WI, 1993; *Forensic Accounting Handbook, 2nd edition*, Assets Protection Publishing, Madison, WI, 1993; the Executive Protection Manual[1]; and *Corporate Crime Investigation*, Butterworth-Heinemann, Boston, 1997. He is the author of *Managing Legal and Security Risks in Computing and Communications*, Butterworth-Heinemann, Boston, 1998.

---

[1] Motorola Teleprograms, Inc., 1976. *Executive Protection Manual*, Chicago.

PREFACE

RESPONSIBILITIES AND WEAPONS

If you are a small businessperson, you are well aware of the many meanings attached to the word *responsibility*. The phrase fiduciary responsibility has probably been mentioned by your banker when he or she either turned down or gave you a loan. Your accountant has told you of your responsibility to keep all your receipts and records (especially mileage) and to record everything accurately. Your employees have mentioned now and then about the direction and opportunities for the company under responsible management.

Now, in addition to growing your company, paying its bills, and keeping yourself employed, you have a new responsibility: protecting your company.

You always knew that. However, things have changed. You've become computerized. These weirdos you've heard of in the news or seen on television and the things they do—breaking into computer systems for fun, or maybe dropping a virus into a network that spans the globe, or maybe grabbing a few million dollars from a bank with a phony wire transfer.

Maybe you wonder how much money someone in your company could steal with a wire transfer. Could anyone at work do that? Do you have insurance to cover that? With those thoughts, you've started a journey.

By getting computers and networks, then getting on the Web and setting up your own Website, you've become a member of Cyberland. Now we would like to introduce you to one of the malignancies afoot in this once relatively pastoral outland—cybercrime; and its practitioners, cybercriminals. Major causes of the increase in cybercrime are employees who understand computers and security—and owners and managers who don't.

The major threat to computer systems is usually portrayed in the media as the outsider: the technologically sophisticated hacker who can defeat virtually any security system. However, the real concern for large and small businesses is the insider: the employee, consultant, contractor, or customer who may have ready access to your system. Numerous reputable surveys and studies, and the author's over thirty years' experience in assets protection, lead to the conclusion that at least 75 percent of computer-related crime is committed by insiders.

Cyberfraud is a crime that is perpetrated, aided, or abetted most often by technology specialists in information systems. The definition covers computer-related crime, theft of proprietary information, electronic intrusion, credit card fraud, embezzlement, extortion, and sabotage. Small businesses face an increased threat from cybercrime because they are becoming more dependent on computing and communication systems. In addition, small companies often lack the resources and expertise needed to devise adequate protection measures.

Cyberfraud in Small Businesses: What Auditors and Owners Need to Know is written for the owner, manager, or auditor of a small business or organization. *Cyberfraud* covers threats and vulnerabilities small businesses face from cybercrime. The book describes cost-effective and comprehensive assets protection measures including risk assessments, policies, internal controls, security systems, audits, investigations, and insurance coverage.

It is management's responsibility to understand the company's vulnerabilities, potential threats, warning signs, "red flags," and to establish appropriate protection. Key defenses against computer crime and liability all flow from the owners and managers of the company and their fiduciary duty to protect all significant, valuable assets—financial, physical, and intellectual—from unauthorized use. Management must believe that computer-related crime exists and that their company could become a victim. They must realize that controls and security can reduce the opportunity for crime and that these need to be monitored and enforced.

Management should also be cognizant of the liability that can attach to the organization and its personnel from not taking steps to deter and detect computer crime. Failure to protect assets could leave officers or owners open to charges of contributory negligence should a critical loss occur. Along with this is usually negative publicity and a resulting loss of business.

Owners and managers must know when and where to seek outside advice and expertise, and the critical questions to ask of specific advisors, including an attorney, an insurance agent, an accountant or auditor, a security consultant or investigator, and a computer security specialist.

Cyberfraud provides the small businessperson with a set of questions and talking points for each of the above advisors. Appendices to the book include an overview of the various laws covering computer crime, intellectual property, workplace and employee problems, tort law covering negligence and liability, and compliance programs.

Adrian, Michigan   G. Jack Bologna
May 2000   Paul Shaw

CONTENTS

CONTENTS

AVOIDING CYBERFRAUD IN SMALL BUSINESSES

1

CYBERFRAUD IS
HERE TO STAY

In the old days when computer crimes were being committed by programmers, analysts, data entry clerks, and hackers, the general public showed no great concern or alarm. But even then, data security managers saw a far more serious risk looming as computer technology became cheaper and simpler and as information systems became more accessible to more people.

EARLY COMPUTER-RELATED FRAUDS

The computer frauds discovered in earlier days were sometimes ingenious but rarely expensive from the cash point of view. New buzzwords entered the criminal lexicon to describe these high tech crimes, terms like trap doors, Trojan horses, salami-slicing and superzapping. Still, the public showed no great concern. A few (poorly drafted) computer crime laws were passed and everyone hoped that now the problem of high-technology crime would go away.

But the problem hasn't died down or gone away, nor is it likely to stop anytime soon. Cybercrime is here to stay. Why? Because there is a lot of money to be made in it and the probability of being caught is very low.

Theoretically, there are several layers and types of control that are intended to deter and detect high-tech crimes (i.e., audit controls and organizational controls). They rest on the theory that general managers and accountants are more knowledgeable about defenses to fraud, theft, and embezzlement than designing, corrupt, or incompetent employees are knowledgeable about offensive methods to compromise systems of control. Experience and logic suggest the opposite. Defense follows offense; the criminal mind always has a lead point of time. The critical question is: Has the application of modern technology to accounting systems provided more lead time to the criminal? If so, the social threat today from cybercrime is greater than at any time in the past.

Look at a couple of computer crimes of the past for perspective. The granddaddy of computer-related crimes is the Equity Funding case, a situation in which an insurance company deceived its stockholders for many years by falsely representing its revenues and profits. Both were grossly over-inflated; revenues were over-inflated to the tune of $200,000,000. The technique used to inflate revenues was simple enough. The company merely stated it had sold more insurance policies than it had in fact. The ploy used to deceive company auditors consisted of generating fictitious policies on fictitious people. This went on for five years and involved a total of 200 company employees, including top managers, most of the data processing staff, and even an outside auditor.

Why was the fraud so difficult to detect? With a conspiracy of such large and diverse proportions, how could any mortal auditor discover the fraud? In fact, the fraud was brought to a head only when a disgruntled employee left the firm and blew the whistle to an investment advisor whose clients had a fair-sized stake in the company. The auditor, in turn, advised the Securities Exchange Commission (SEC).

Other reasons for the difficulty in detecting the fraud were:

- Audit tools then available were inadequate.
- Auditors were not knowledgeable enough about auditing in a computerized accounting environment.
- Auditors were inadequately trained by their firms and poorly educated by their colleges.
- Auditors were not equipped to deal with the fast-changing world of financial services.

These are rather serious charges, but Equity Funding took place in the late 1960s and early 1970s. We've come a long way since then, right? Yes, we have, but so has computer technology. Unfortunately, the gap between computer technology and audit, accounting, and management controls hasn't shrunk at all. If anything, the gap has grown.

Take as another example, the Volkswagen case, where it appears that some person or persons inside Volkswagen and perhaps outside the firm, manipulated its accounting records to cover up trading losses on foreign currencies to the tune of $259 million. The losses occurred in 1984 but went undiscovered until late 1986 or early 1987. How was this possible? Again, how sophisticated was its accounting system? Was it auditable? How well-educated and -trained were its auditors? And the critical question, "Did technology inspire the crime?" While the facts indicate that this case involved incompetence or bad luck more than it did an evil intention to steal money from the company, technology provided a method to cover up the fraud.

COMPUTERS AS A TARGET FOR TERRORISTS

Political terrorists, extremists, and protest groups often have common traits, such as tactical use of violence, attempted media manipulation, ideologies, causes, and enemies. But these similarities often can be superficial and misleading.

Most radical groups of the past adopted a revolutionary ideology derived from left-wing socialism or communism. Right-wing groups lean toward fascist or neo-nazi ideas. Today's radical protester is often part of a "social justice movement." He or she may be in an animal rights or an earth-liberation group. Members at the fringe of these groups have earned the moniker "eco-terrorists" by destroying labs that use animals in experiments or burning down a ski resort that might destroy a habitat for endangered species. Free software advocates have their fringe members who may be inclined to attack information systems.

Political or social terrorism is a strategy of intimidation and coercion—through the tactical use of, or threat to use, illegitimate force (such as sabotage)—to influence the political, social, or commercial behavior of an opponent or to provoke fear or respect from the general population. Terrorism is not mindless violence, nor is it irrational, though it often seems so. Terrorists have objectives for their actions.

In the dramaturgy of terror there must be a transgressor/victim, terrorist, and audience. Terrorists distinguish between violent (it used to be called armed) propaganda and regular propaganda. With violent propaganda, the act of terror itself is the vehicle that carries the message to the audience.

Terrorists usually have one or more objectives behind their propaganda:

- To advertise the existence of a group
- To publicize the group's cause
- To create an atmosphere of disorientation, fear, and alarm
- To portray their acts as the lesser evil (e.g., destroy a specific piece of property vs. allowing the destruction of a habitat)
- To extort specific concessions from a specific target—stop abortions, get off the land, provide publicity for a manifesto

Many extremists have accepted the premise that violent and unlawful threats and acts are justified if they promote their program to change society—for the better, of course. Extremists and protest groups must propagandize—usually by deed—if they are to gain active or tacit support for their cause. Today's radical has a wealth of past experience and information to draw on, regarding strategy, tactics, or practical advice. As long as there is television and other news media, there will be radicals who will manipulate it to their purposes.

THE DILEMMA OF ELECTRONIC COMMERCE

More and more companies, large and small, are deploying Web-based, electronic commerce applications for competitive advantage and a good return on investment. These systems must be customer-friendly, with service centers providing access for order entry, inventory status, shipping instructions, or delivery schedule. The challenge for a market-driven system is controlling costs/increasing profits vs. protecting proprietary information.

Fifteen Reasons Why Cyberfraud Is Here to Stay

1. Growing use of personal computers and communications devices connected with computers make security measures difficult.

2. Valuable proprietary information has become more vulnerable to theft with the move away from protected mainframes to less secure decentralized networks of personal computers.

6

3. Current popular software is designed primarily for ease of use; security was not seen as a desired feature.

4. Computer hackers have new tools—data dictionaries and hacking software to uncover computer access passwords stored in a system.

5. Information and communications systems change rapidly, making security upgrades costly and often difficult to implement.

6. New or upgraded computer systems often take a productivity toll and alienate employees.

7. The importance of compliance with information protection policies and measures is often poorly communicated to employees.

8. A business strategy rooted in constant productivity sees security as slowing down the job.

9. As information technology systems get more complex, security also becomes complicated and layered with slower authorization procedures, thus wasting a lot of high-paid time.

10. Practices of open management and teams call for access to and sharing of proprietary information among employees, increasing potential important information losses.

11. Many employees are not willing to follow security procedures, preferring routine and convenience.

12. At a small company, the atmosphere regarding computer crime is often "it can't happen to us."

13. There will always be disaffected people and some will surely find reasons to see a company's computer system as the cause of their problem and take destructive retaliation against the company.

14. New generations of cyberpunks will see the computer system as a complex security labyrinth waiting to be invaded.

15. Business ethics appear to be eroding.

Cyberfraud will continue to grow until we shift from a crisis mode of audit and control to a prevention mode. Prevention means awareness, education, training, early involvement of auditors in design of new systems, and an effort to make these security systems an integral part of the computing infrastructure.

Even doing all of the above won't solve cyberfraud completely. It will, however, minimize the potential for the occurrence of cyberfraud and maximize the potential of the perpetrator being caught.

2

CYBERCRIME AND CYBERCRIMINALS

Cybercrime or computer-related crime, abuse and misuse, can be summed up in a concept called MOMMs, Motivations (why), Opportunities (when), Methods (where), and Means (how).

MOTIVATIONS

The motivations for computer-related crimes are in order of frequency:

1. Economic
2. Egocentric
3. Ideological
4. Psychotic

The economic motive for computer crime is the easiest to understand. The criminal wants and takes something of value which belongs to another.

The egocentric motive involves a desire on the part of the culprit to prove or demonstrate that he or she is not a victim of technology but indeed has mastered it well enough to sabotage or compromise it. The act of damage or theft is not intended to enrich the culprit so much as it is to show off his or her technical prowess. Such criminals are often caught because they can't seem to restrain the temptation to openly boast about their accomplishment.

The compulsive cyberpunk is an egocentric. Kevin Mitnick, charged and convicted in 1989 of unauthorized invasion of a computer database, is an example. It has been said of Mitnick that he couldn't let a day go by without proving that he could bypass a security system and get into a database or network system.

Ideologically motivated computer criminals tend to be members of extremist groups employing violence and extortion to further their political, religious, or social goals. Of course, many protestors have used tactics that come under malicious mischief or breaking and entering laws. Other protestors, however, have wreaked destruction on laboratories, computer centers, and threatened and intimidated professionals into abandoning research programs.

Some people may feel that technology is oppressing them or invading their privacy, degenerating the society as a whole, or that all software should be free. They may seek to wreak revenge on their oppressors by terrorist actions against computer systems or tele-communications networks. Their act is tantamount to a strong statement of dissatisfaction with things as they are, or an act which they hope will evoke media attention to their causes or beliefs. Spite, hate, and anger tend to be their motivations for theft, sabotage, or extortion.

Psychotic criminal acts may be the result of a distorted sense of reality, delusions of persecution, obsessions, or compulsions.

OPPORTUNITIES

Computer crimes usually arise because of inadequacies in the workplace which provide the opportunities for crime or abuse:

Systems Controls

Systems controls are vulnerable when internal accounting, audit, and/or administrative controls are inadequate or when access control systems are lax or absent.

Management Controls

Management controls are vulnerable when the work and ethical environments of the firm are inadequate (i.e., standards, procedures, and policies are undocumented, ambivalent, or contradictory).

A poor climate for interpersonal trust also causes vulnerability. A poor climate is exhibited by excessive employee or management rivalry or competitiveness, punitiveness, and unequal or biased treatment of personnel.

METHODS

This book has thus far discussed the motivation and opportunity aspects of computer-related crime, but committing a computer crime requires motivations, opportunities, and means.

MEANS

Means and opportunities tend to be interrelated with conditions in the work environment. The means for carrying out a computer crime involves the exploitation of weaknesses in:

- *Controls.* Bypassing or overriding controls, counterfeiting or destroying data input or output documents
- *Personnel.* Enlisting other employees into a criminal conspiracy
- *Technological skills.* Effecting the use of viruses, worms, Trojan horses, etc.

METHODS

The methods for committing computer crimes have been classified into input scams, throughput scams, and output scams.

Input scams involve the manipulation, alteration, or fabrication of data before or during its entry into a computer. Input scams are probably the most common computer-related crimes and yet the easiest to prevent with effective supervision and controls (i.e., separation of duties, audit trails, control totals, parity checks, limit checks, and access controls).

Throughput scams require knowledge of programming. Such colorful expressions as salami slicing, Trojan horses, worms, trap doors, time bombs, logic bombs, and viruses have been used to describe these computer abuses.

Output scams include the theft of computer-generated reports and proprietary information files, or the theft of computer time/service.

The chief culprits of input and output are employee insiders.

Computer crime and abuse arises when motivations and opportunity exist, and the cybercriminal has sufficient knowledge and skills (means) to carry it out. The variable factors here are motivations and means. Opportunities are the least variable because there are no foolproof controls systems. All computer systems have weaknesses which can be compromised.

CYBERCRIMES: INSIDERS vs. OUTSIDERS

Insiders

The ratio of insiders to outsiders committing computer-related crimes is believed by some computer security experts to be as high as 80 percent to 20 percent. Certainly, insiders pose the greatest threat since they usually possess two crucial kinds of knowledge needed to carry out a successful cybercrime:

1. *Technical knowledge.* How the computer, communications, and security system operates

2. *Operational knowledge.* How the business operates, accounting practices, security and auditing procedures, and financial processes

Let's look at the embezzler in some detail to see how this consummate insider/thief uses computer skills coupled with information on a company's financial operations to commit a crime.

Computers offer embezzlers with some computing and accounting skills an easier way to steal and make their crime harder to detect and prosecute. Embezzlers are often the ultimate insiders in a small company. Employers enhance the opportunity for embezzlement by having most or all financial operations on the computer, putting one person in charge, and having lax internal financial controls or none at all. All an embezzler needs is control of the computer or one or more of its financial operations, such as payroll or accounts payable.

Computer-related embezzlement schemes differ from other embezzlement methods in at least one important regard. The use of computer systems makes it possible for thieves to steal more money faster and to leave comparatively little evidence of their acts.

Successful embezzlers attempt to make their fraudulent entries look or appear normal by any control criteria. The amount will be within established limits, the entry originator will be authorized and account classifications will be proper. The place and timing of the transaction will be appropriate as will the transacting parties. The subject matter of the transaction will be fitting to the needs of the business.

FEATURES OF COMPUTER-RELATED EMBEZZLEMENT SCHEMES

Other criminals find clever ways to manipulate weaknesses in the accounting and control systems so that their peculations appear to be within the bounds of the weak standards, policies, procedures, and exceptions criteria.

To cover up their activities, for example, embezzlers typically create misinformation or disinformation, destroy or suppress information, or utilize rationalizations if authenticity or accuracy of an entry is challenged. They dream up stories that can justify their entries and thereby create a form of plausible deniability.

FOUR DISTINCTIVE FEATURES OF COMPUTER-RELATED EMBEZZLEMENT SCHEMES

1. They are committed generally by people with suitable skills in computer operations or information systems auditing. However, it is possible for someone completely unskilled in computing to steal significant amounts of funds from an information processing application.

2. They are carried out most often by exploiting deficiencies in an application's existing internal controls. These weaknesses may stem from defects in the design or installation of the controls themselves, negligence in consistent enforcement or a failure to monitor and follow up expeditiously on their operation.

3. Computer-related embezzlements can be executed at any of the three stages of the transaction processing flow, input, throughput, or output. The most common uncovered thefts are those executed in the input stage, during which false, forged, or altered data is entered.

4. Most commonly, these embezzlement schemes are directed against accounts payable, payroll, and benefit or expense claims.

Primary insider threats come from information technology specialists with unique skills, access to systems, and user trust. Potential positions are systems administrators, computer security personnel, programmers, or network engineers.

Insiders are often employees who are technology specialists with special skills and access who become angry or disgruntled over professional slights and failures, lack of praise, a feeling of betrayal, being cheated out of job advancement, harassment, or boredom. They can resort to sabotage, theft, and extortion of the organization's computer system, data, or proprietary information.

OUTSIDERS

The most well-known outsider is the hacker, adept at penetrating any computer system and crashing it, browsing anywhere, planting nefarious code, or doing whatever else pleases him or her. Hackers may see themselves as Robin Hood, Che Guevera, or Willy Sutton. It is an image that attracts the media and for those with a cause, it is a new variation of the propaganda of the deed.

Of course, there are pure criminals after money, credit card numbers, and financial transaction data and there are sure to be terrorist organizations bent on knocking out a computer controlling a power grid.

Companies, especially smaller ones, should spend their limited security money mostly countering vulnerabilities from employees, rather than technological threats posed by outsiders.

ANSWERS TO SOME MYTHS ABOUT CYBERCRIME

Are most computer thefts discovered by accident rather than audit or design features in the software or hardware? No. We would suggest the following is closer to the truth:

1. Systems, controls, and countermeasures inhibit, thwart, deter, and detect computer-related theft, fraud, embezzlement, and information piracy in 20 percent or more of the possible incidents.

2. The value which a society places on such virtues as personal honesty and integrity will discourage another 20 percent of the possible computer abuse cases.

3. The value which a firm places on honesty, integrity, and personal trust will discourage 20 percent more.

4. Fear of apprehension and incarceration will effect another 20 percent reduction in the possible incidents.

5. Nothing will discourage the other 20 percent. They will lie, cheat, steal, embezzle, or sabotage for reasons which often defy rational analysis.

Unfortunately, as thieves are more exciting, interesting, and noteworthy than computer security, they get media attention.

While the authors don't believe that movies or TV shows provide motives for crime, they do believe that they provide convenient rationalizations for criminals to justify their crime under a veil of self-righteousness or intellectual arrogance. In fact, the country seems to be brimming with self-righteous people and groups, as well as those who want all information to be free, with intellectual property laws repealed in the name of fairness.

Today, who would be foolish enough to assure management that theft, fraud, or embezzlement are unlikely events in the company? Society can't survive without standards and ethical norms and the same is true for a company—management must set ethical policies and examples of ethical behavior. This is the "tone at the top" concept: Employees will watch and emulate. Computer security awareness and training can build on this.

Another area of improvement is the removal of some destructive notions. Some old views about computer crime should be restructured as follows:

1. Most computer thieves are really stupid and eventually get caught.

2. Most computer frauds never get beyond the imagination stage before the perpetrator discovers a weakness in the plan and gives it up.

3. Most computer thieves fail to prepare a suitable alibi before, or an adequate defense after, their crimes are committed and rarely "beat the rap."

SUMMARY

Exhibit 2.1 depicts computer-related theft as an iterative process.

EXHIBIT 2.1
The Computer Theft Iteration

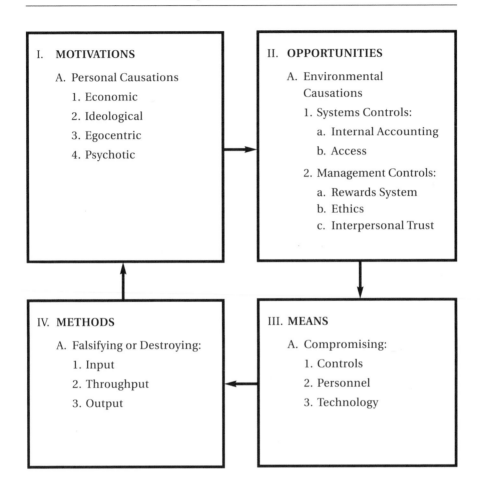

I. **MOTIVATIONS**

   A. Personal Causations

      1. Economic

      2. Ideological

      3. Egocentric

      4. Psychotic

II. **OPPORTUNITIES**

   A. Environmental Causations

      1. Systems Controls:

         a. Internal Accounting

         b. Access

      2. Management Controls:

         a. Rewards System

         b. Ethics

         c. Interpersonal Trust

IV. **METHODS**

   A. Falsifying or Destroying:

      1. Input

      2. Throughput

      3. Output

III. **MEANS**

   A. Compromising:

      1. Controls

      2. Personnel

      3. Technology

3

RISK AND VULNERABILITY ASSESSMENTS

Risk is the chance of loss or exposure to a peril. A pure risk, such as the risk of theft or sabotage, embodies only the possibility of loss. This chapter examines pure risks as well as:

- *Risk control.* The identification, analysis, measurement, and elimination, reduction, or avoidance of risk

- *Risk analysis.* The identification of risk factors, followed by measurement or estimation to determine possible loss frequency or severity

- *Risk exposure survey.* An inventory of loss exposure possibilities; this is an ongoing process with emphasis on evaluation, experience, and judgment

- *Risk management.* The encompassing process of risk exposure identification, the judgmental analysis of risk, and the control or elimination of risk.

Before a discussion of more formal risk analysis, let's examine a few sure things. First, the highest pure risk is going to be internal. The threat is from employees or contractors who know the computer system. They know the system's vulnerabilities, which failures would create the biggest problems or cause the most damage. They may have broad or selective security clearance, and they are trusted.

The assets at greatest risk will vary with the company, but computer-related assets are information that concerns business operations, systems that process electronic commerce, finance, manufacturing, distribution, marketing, and human resources. Strategic planning or research and development (R & D) information may also be included. Losses in these areas may not be limited to money, but may include employee privacy, morale, and reputational damage.

A RISK-RANKING TECHNIQUE

A risk-ranking system can analyze an automated financial management system in terms of relative risk, specifically its vulnerability to fraud, abuse, mismanagement, and internal control. The ranking procedure is a three-step approach:

1. Evaluation of each system in terms of risk factors and assignment of a numeric risk value for each factor: 3—high, 2—medium, 1—low.

2. Assign an importance weight to each factor and compute a composite numerical score for each system.

3. Rank the systems in order of vulnerability based on the composite scores.

For example, Exhibit 3.1 contains a list of factors that should be considered in developing the ranking. While other system-specific factors may be considered in determining vulnerability, these factors provide a reasonable and efficient framework for an audit review.

Assign weights to each ranking factor based on their relative importance in assessing risk. These weights should be developed by rating each factor in order of importance on a scale of one to five based on prior experience in reviewing accounting systems and internal controls. To develop a composite score for each system, the weights are multiplied by the risk-ranking values and the products totaled.

The risk factors contained in Exhibit 3.1 are explained as follows:

- *Purpose of the system.* A high-risk system is critical to controlling the use of funds and other operating resources, where exposure to loss or disruption could cripple operations. Accounting systems may be ranked medium. Systems that only record and report summary financial data, which are not crucial to operations, may be ranked low.

EXHIBIT 3.1
Worksheet for Preparing
Computer Systems Risk Ranking Scores

Factor	Risk	× Weight	= Composite Score
Purpose of system	____	_____	_____
System documentation	____	_____	_____
Dollar volume controlled by the system	____	_____	_____
Verification of input	____	_____	_____
Number of dependent systems	____	_____	_____
Amount of computer resources used	____	_____	_____
Known system problems	____	_____	_____
Recency of audit	____	_____	_____
Legal requirements met	____	_____	_____
Involvement of users and auditors in system design	____	_____	_____
		TOTAL	_____

- *System documentation.* Documentation ensures system maintenance and operation; little or no documentation would give a system a high-risk ranking. A medium-risk system is one with documentation complete except for recent changes. A low-risk system has full documentation during development and subsequent changes.

- *Dollar volume controlled by the system.* In general, the greater the dollar volume or transactions in a system, the higher its risk ranking. However, the ranking should be determined on a system-by-system basis.

- *Verification of input.* The ability of a system to verify the accuracy of input data determines the risk ranking. Data received only from outside the organization sources, whose accuracy cannot be verified with company-generated data, gets a high risk. A medium risk is given to the system if the input data from sources outside the company can be independently verified as to accuracy. A low risk should be given if the data is received from sources within the company and the system can verify its accuracy with other company-generated data.

- *Number of other dependent systems.* A system with several dependent systems may be ranked high. A medium applies when only one dependent system exists. A solo operation gets a low ranking.

- *Amount of computer resources used.* High usage equals high risk and low computer resource usage equals low risk. This is a judgment call based on the company's total computer resources.

- *Known system problems.* Previously identified significant system problems may hinder the system from meeting its stated goals imply a high-risk ranking. A medium ranking applies if the problems do not prevent the system from meeting its goals. If no problems were turned up by previous audits or inspections, a low ranking applies.

- *Recency of audit.* Systems which have never been audited get a high-risk ranking. A full-scope audit within the last two years would give the system a low ranking. Systems with limited scope audits or audits that were performed two and five years ago should be ranked medium.

- *Legal and compliance requirements met.* A high rating applies if the system is relied on for meeting compliance program standards or with statutes or regulations. A low one is given if no regulatory or statutory requirements exist.

- *Involvement of users, compliance officer, legal counsel, and auditors in systems design.* A high-risk ranking applies if neither users nor auditors were involved in setting system design and internal controls. If such participation took place, a system should get a low-risk ranking. If only the users or the auditors participated, the system would be ranked medium.

VULNERABILITY ASSESSMENTS

A vulnerability assessment reviews the susceptibility of a computer system or function to the occurrence of waste, loss, unauthorized use, or misappropriation. More specifically, a vulnerability assessment is intended to determine the likelihood that situations exist in which:

- Use of or access to the computer or network are not in compliance with applicable law.

- Funds, property, and other assets are not adequately safeguarded against waste, loss, unauthorized use, or misappropriation.

- Revenues and expenditures applicable to company operations are not properly recorded and accounted for and therefore do not permit the preparation of accounts and reliable financial reports or the maintenance of accountability over assets.

However, the internal control evaluation process does not stop with vulnerability assessments since, by themselves, vulnerability assessments do not necessarily identify weaknesses or result in improvements. Rather, vulnerability assessments are the mechanisms with which a company can determine the relative potential for loss, abuse, or misuse of computer systems. Then, the company may schedule internal control reviews, security surveys, or related actions.

A vulnerability assessment consists of the following three steps:

1. Analysis of the general control environment

2. Analysis of inherent risk

3. Preliminary evaluation of safeguards

Analysis of General Control Environment

The environment in which activities are conducted has a major impact on the effectiveness of internal control within a company. Several factors determine the general control environment:

- *Management attitude.* Management recognition of the importance of and commitment to the establishment and maintenance of a strong system of internal control as communicated to employees through actions and words
- *Organizational structure.* The identification of organizational units to perform the necessary functions and the establishment of appropriate reporting relationships
- *Personnel.* The competence and integrity of the organization's personnel
- *Delegation and communication of authority and responsibility.* Appropriate delegation or limitation of authority in a manner that provides assurance that responsibilities are effectively discharged
- *Policies and procedures.* The definition, documentation, and dissemination of information to all employees as to how the organization is intended to perform in various situations
- *Budgeting and reporting practices.* The specification and communication of organizational goals and the extent of their accomplishment
- *Organizational checks and balances.* The establishment of an appropriate level of financial and other management controls and internal auditing
- *Information technology consideration.* An awareness of the strengths and exposures inherent in computer and communications systems and the existence of appropriate controls

Controls

Questions to ask regarding controls include:

- What are the weakest links in the system's chain of internal controls?
- What deviations from conventional good accounting practices are possible in this system?

- How are off-line transactions handled and who can authorize such transactions?
- What control features in the system can be bypassed or over-ridden by high authorities?
- How often has this happened or is it happening now?
- Who is involved?
- What rationale have they advanced for such variances and deviations?
- How generally well-known are such exceptions among the organization's employees?
- Are cash, receivables, inventories, and payables building up or diminishing?
- Are receivables write-offs building up?
- Are inventory reclassifications building up? For example, are reclassifications from merchandise or finished goods available for sale, or are they obsolete, scrap, damaged, or sample status?
- Are the company's products or services on the wane? Are sales down markedly? Is the industry itself on the wane? How do company sales compare with its main competitors?
- What is the past relationship between inventory and accounts receivable buildup, between sales, inventory, and receivables buildup; between payables and inventory buildups? Have there been any material changes recently in these relationships?

An evaluation of the general control environment is the first step in the vulnerability assessment process. It should be performed by determining whether the characteristics of a strong general control environment, as described above, exist by reviewing documented policies and procedures; talking with management and other personnel; observing practices; and drawing upon a familiarity with the operation.

Analyses of Inherent Risk

The second step in the vulnerability assessment process is the performance of an analysis for each identified system and administrative function. The analyses should check for the inherent potential for waste, loss, unauthorized use, or misappropriation due to the nature of the activity itself.

Purpose and characteristics. The purpose and characteristics of program or administrative functions should be considered, and any aspects that make the activity susceptible to waste, loss, unauthorized use, or misappropriation noted. The following matters should be noted, particularly since they often tend to contribute to fraud, waste, and abuse:

- Broad or vague missions, goals or objectives
- High degree of complexity
- Activities operating under severe time constraints
- Activities involving the handling of cash receipts

Prior reviews. Prior audit reports, internal evaluations, and consulting reports should be reviewed for any indications that the system or administrative function has previously been subject to losses due to waste, loss, unauthorized use, or misappropriation. The amounts of estimated losses, if any, and the period covered by the prior review should be considered.

Programs or functions with minimal audit coverage or with significant and repeated findings should be considered more susceptible to waste, loss, unauthorized use, or misappropriation.

Management responsiveness. Management's responsiveness to recommendations from its evaluation groups should be considered. This would include actions taken to correct problems brought to management's attention as a result of prior reviews. A lack of responsiveness suggests a higher degree of susceptibility to waste, loss, unauthorized use, or misappropriation.

Preliminary Evaluation of Security

The third step in the vulnerability assessment process is the making of a preliminary judgment regarding the existence and adequacy of internal control over specific computer systems and administrative functions. The key consideration should be whether appropriate controls are in place to prevent or at least minimize waste, loss, unauthorized use, or misappropriation. A preliminary evaluation should contain seven steps:

VULNERABILITY ASSESSMENTS

1. Review/inspect terrain and topography of the site: fencing, lighting, guardposts, parking areas, shipping, receiving, staging and storage areas, intrusion alarm systems, access and egress procedures, doors, locks, windows, surveillance equipment, and patrol methodology.

2. Review personnel policies, practices, procedures and priorities with respect to employee honesty, such as management's philosophy toward its human resources, recruitment and selection standards, termination policies, development and promotion policies and practices.

3. Review information handling, classification and protection practices, policies, and procedures to determine their adequacy.

4. Review inventory and property accounting controls (raw materials, finished goods, parts, small tools, and portable equipment).

5. Review cash and securities handling practices, procedures and policies, authorizations, and other controls.

6. Review computing and communications systems to determine adequacy of physical security safeguards, disaster/recovery plans, information protection practices, and telecommunications security.

7. Review the past history of the firm with respect to critical incidents which have security implications (i.e., past thefts of property and proprietary information by employees).

As stated, an in-depth review of the existing controls is not appropriate at this stage. Rather, the evaluator's judgment should be based largely on his or her knowledge of the existence and functioning of safeguards that protect the company's resources from waste, loss, unauthorized use, or mismanagement. However, the evaluation must be thoughtful and based on a working knowledge of the computer system or administrative function. Judgments made without knowledge of the situation are usually not sufficiently reliable.

SUMMARIZING THE RESULTS OF THE VULNERABILITY ASSESSMENTS

The completion of the three steps permits the assessor to make an overall assessment of the adherence of the program or administrative function's internal control system to at least some of the prescribed internal standards. It also leads to an assessment of the vulnerability of the program or administrative function itself. The assessment should be documented and a conclusion reached as to overall vulnerability. See Exhibit 3.2 for a sample vulnerability chart.

Problems or weaknesses requiring immediate corrective action may be observed during the performance of the vulnerability assessments. For instance, a program may be assessed in which the controls are perceived to be grossly inadequate and there is a strong possibility of loss if corrective action is not taken immediately.

DEVELOPING A PLAN FOR SUBSEQUENT ACTIONS

The next step in the process is to use the summarized vulnerability assessments to determine appropriate subsequent actions. It is important at this point to remember the overall objective of the internal control evaluation process. This is to bring about a strengthening of internal control systems in a cost-effective manner.

One approach may be to classify the vulnerability of each of the programs and administrative functions subject to these guidelines to facilitate the establishment of a prioritized schedule for internal control reviews. Highly vulnerable functions would require a detailed review of internal controls. Moderately vulnerable activities would permit less intensive and less frequent internal control reviews. See Exhibit 3.3 for a sample Control Evaluation Form.

Another approach would be to consider a series of options for each of the program and administrative functions. This could be done by first evaluating the degree and causes of the vulnerabilities; then considering management priorities, resource availability, and other management initiatives underway. Finally, appropriate courses of action could be determined. These might consist of:

- Scheduling and conducting an internal control review
- Requesting an audit

EXHIBIT 3.2
Sample Vulnerability Chart

Asset			Individual With Access to Asset	Method of Theft/Fraud	Controls		Concealment		Conversion	
At Risk	Monetary Value	Attractiveness			In Effect	Effectiveness	Methods	Probability	Methods	Probability

EXHIBIT 3.3
Control Evaluation Form

CONTROL	CONCLUSION				EXPLANATION	RECOMMENDATIONS
	good	adequate	poor	absent		

- Establishing increased or improved monitoring procedures
- Developing and conducting training programs for the staff
- Issuing clarifying instructions
- Modifying procedures or documents

An approach such as the latter can help to ensure that resources devoted to the internal control evaluation and improvement process are used in an effective and efficient manner.

4

ASSESSING
FIDELITY RISKS

The protection and preservation of a firm's assets (human, capital, technological, and information) from the foreseeable consequences of acts of God (climatic catastrophes), and acts of the public enemy (property theft, fraud, embezzlement, sabotage, information piracy, or commercial corruption) are the peculiar responsibility of a company's officers, directors, managers, and agents, whose authority is based on a host of federal, state, and local laws, as well as the general common law of contracts, agency, torts, and fiduciary responsibility.

The risk of liability for not having adequate security—whether for premises, websites, or data processing systems—is destined to rise. It should be noted that the Association of Trial Lawyers of America has formed the Inadequate Security Litigation Group. Litigation and awards have both increased dramatically.

The question of how much is "reasonable" security will most often be left to juries to decide. This will place the burden on the defendant to present evidence that either the act was not foreseeable (such as a totally random act) or that security was adequate. The ability to foresee a crime increases the defendant/owner's duty; the likelihood of a crime is foreseeable, for example, if there were past occurrences.

In the present litigious situation, it is a good idea to document your security measures and maintain an awareness of the basic legal elements of the tort of negligence.

Officers and directors of public companies are now keenly aware of these responsibilities. The point is often brought home to them by actions initiated by the Securities Exchange Commission (SEC); also by lawsuits initiated by irate stockholders and creditors, employees, environmentalists, state and local authorities, and community organizations. Officers and directors must therefore exercise discretion, good business judgment, and due diligence in their management of company assets and business operations. Any failure in exercising care may subject them to lawsuits by damaged parties. The exercise of prudent business judgment would therefore dictate that enlightened top management undertake a serious review of the adequacy of asset protection plans, policies, procedures, and controls.

Such a review is important for several reasons. First, as a defensive measure, to assure top management that reasonable and adequate precautions have in fact been taken. Second, as a prevention measure, to detect new areas of control weaknesses and vulnerabilities that may require administrative action or correction. Third, it is an offensive measure to reduce losses and insurance premiums.

One area of growing top management concern is employee honesty. Industries with high risks of loss from employee dishonesty include banks, insurance carriers, stockbrokers, gambling casinos, and many types of retail establishments that accumulate large sums of cash. Since cash is so easy to dispose of, these industries tend to be the hardest hit by employee infidelity. But there are other forms of infidelity beyond theft of cash, such as theft or embezzlement or destruction of other company assets and defrauding the company, unauthorized disclosure of trade secrets, and corruption by vendors.

Large or small businesses should perhaps form a risk assessment team to conduct the periodic reviews of asset protection plans, policies, procedures, practices, and controls mentioned above.

What should such a review encompass? Such a review is in effect an evaluation of the adequacy of controls and protection measures. Are the safeguards commensurate with the degree of risk? Are they cost-effective? Do they minimize or optimize risk?

INFIDELITY CAUSATION VARIABLES

Employee fidelity is a product of several causation variables, in the following order of importance:

1. The integrity of the individual employees, such as values, beliefs, and attitudes (pre- and post-employment character)

2. The culture of the organization (ethical and motivational climate)

3. The character and culture of the employee's co-workers (peer pressures)

4. The prevailing social values and mores in the geographical areas in which the company does business (is infidelity fashionable?)

5. The level of ethical conduct in the industry of which the organization is a member

6. The security and control policies, plans, and procedures of the organization (not enough = infidelity threat; too much = invitation to retaliate for feelings of oppression). Is the organization ruled by reason or by fear? Has the ruler abdicated his authority? Is the rabble in command?

WHEN EMPLOYEE INFIDELITY IS MOST LIKELY TO OCCUR

Infidelity occurs most often when and where:

- Employees are hired without due consideration for their honesty and integrity.
- Employees are poorly managed, exploited, abused, or placed under great stress to accomplish financial goals and objectives.
- Management models are themselves corrupt, inefficient, or incompetent.
- The industry of which the company is a part has a history or tradition of corruption.
- The company has fallen on bad times. It is losing money, or market share; its products or services are becoming passé.

HOW INFIDELITY IS MOST LIKELY TO OCCUR

Physical custody of property, access to accounting records, and knowledge and authority to override controls are the main ingredients of employee fraud, theft, and embezzlement.

People who have access to corporate assets and knowledge of the internal and accounting controls, or who hold management roles of the sort where they can exercise an override of such controls, are in the best position to commit infidelities against their companies. The threat of infidelity is greatest at senior management levels since access to assets and authority to bypass controls is greatest at that level. But infidelity is also a real threat from personnel with accounting, finance, data processing, and property handling responsibilities. They too have access to accounting records and can use that knowledge to compromise controls and access corporate assets.

The most common fraudulent schemes by lower level employees involve cash disbursements, such as phony payables, payroll, benefit, and expense claims. The most common fraudulent schemes by higher level managers involve "profit smoothing" and balance sheet "window dressing," like deferring expenses, booking sales too early, inventory overstatement, asset overstatement, and understatement of liabilities.

TOP MANAGEMENT INFIDELITY

A review of behaviors of corporate defrauders based on some thirty years of personal observation suggests the following as a profile of typical top management defrauders:

- Their personal values tend to be highly economic.
- They tend to live lavishly.
- They are often eccentric in the way they display their wealth or spend their money. They tend to be conspicuous consumers and often boast of the things they have acquired, friends they have in high office, and all of the fine places they have visited.
- Male defrauders tend to adorn their wives with expensive furs and jewelry, usually to compensate for spending so little time with them and their children.
- They often gamble or drink a great deal.
- They are highly self-centered and egocentric.
- Their boasts are not so much about their achievements as about their cunning, and about their winnings rather than their losses.
- They appear to be hard-working, almost compulsive, but most of their time at work is spent in scheming and designing short-cut ways to get ahead or beat off the competition.

- They tend to be late for meetings they scheduled themselves and often leave early or allow themselves to be interrupted by phone calls and private messages to prove their importance.
- They show great hostility toward people who oppose their views or raise objections to their views.
- They tend to treat people as objects, not individuals, and often as objects of exploitation.
- They create a great deal of turnover among their subordinates and often set one subordinate off against another.
- They play favorites among their subordinates, but the relationship can cool very quickly. Subordinates often fall from grace after one mistake, even an insignificant mistake.
- They appear to be reckless or careless with facts and often enlarge on them.
- Typical corporate defrauders manage by crisis more often than by objectives.
- They tend to drift with the tides and have no long-range plans.
- They tend to bypass internal controls with impunity and argue forcefully for less formality in controls.
- They feel exempt from accountability and controls because of their station or position.
- They demand absolute loyalty from subordinates but they themselves are loyal only to their own self-interests.
- They have few real friends within their own industry or company. Their competitors and colleagues usually dislike them.
- In a nutshell, they are motivated by narrow self-interests (economic and egocentric) and not by concern for others, employees, stockholders, customers, or creditors.

LOWER-LEVEL INFIDELITY

What about lower level managers? Are there any behavior indicators at those levels? There are several:

- They feel unduly pressured by their superiors for high performance—higher sales, lower costs, more profits. Top management tolerates no justification or excuse for less than expected or demanded sales, cost, and profit targets. Bonuses are tied to short-term performance levels and don't take economic or competitive realities into consideration.

- They enforce internal controls loosely. They don't want to be bound by them, so why enforce them against subordinates?
- Like their superiors, their business ethics are subordinated to their economic and egocentric self-interests.
- There is a great deal of disorganization and confusion about duties and responsibilities among their subordinates.
- A high level of suspicion and hostility exists among these lower-level managers and their line and staff superiors at headquarters.

EMPLOYEE FIDELITY SURVEY

Internal Threats and Risks: Motivational Environment

1. Do employees have an economic reason to steal from or defraud the company?
   - Are salaries and fringe benefits equitable and competitive with other similar firms in the same market?
   - Are pressures for production and profitable performance so great that people are burning out or becoming disgruntled?
   - Are employee evaluations and salary reviews based on fair and objective criteria?
   - Are promotions based on merit and contribution, and administered fairly, impartially, and openly?
   - Are job-related goals and objectives *imposed* on subordinates or *negotiated* with subordinates?

2. Does the company suffer from a "we-they" syndrome: management versus non-management personnel or middle management versus top management?

3. Do conflicts abound among the top management group over issues that involve corporate philosophy, corporate purpose, corporate direction, or corporate ethics?

4. Is there evidence of spite, hate, hostility, or jealousy among the firm's top management group?

5. Do employees feel oppressed, abused, exploited, or neglected by senior management?

Internal Threats and Risks: Ethical Environment

1. What is the company's past history with respect to:
   - Labor management relations?
   - Turnover of top executives?
   - Moonlighting and conflict of interest by employee and executives?
   - Vandalism, theft, and sabotage by employees?
   - Corruption of customers?
   - Corruption by vendors or competitors?
   - Corruption of labor leaders, regulatory authorities, and political officials?
   - Association of executives with organized crime figures?
   - "High living" by executives?
   - Lack of concern for truth in advertising or selling its products or services?
   - Convictions for business-related crimes?

2. What is the history of the firm and the industry with respect to regulatory compliance?

3. What is the past, current, and future profitability of the firm?

4. Are there any pending litigation and complaints against the firm by regulatory authorities, vendors, customers, creditors, and competitors?

Internal Threats and Risks: Control Environment

1. What are the weakest links in the system's chain of internal controls?

2. What deviations from conventional good accounting practices are possible in this system?

3. How are off-line transactions handled and who can authorize such transactions?

4. What control features in the system can be bypassed or over-ridden by high authorities?
   - How often has this happened or is it happening now?
   - Who is involved?
   - What rationale have they advanced for such variances and deviations?
   - How generally well-known are such exceptions among the organization's employees?

5. Are cash, receivables, inventories, and payables building up or diminishing?

6. Are receivable write-offs building up?

7. Are inventory reclassifications building up? For example, consider reclassifications from merchandise or finished goods available for sale, to obsolete, scrap, damaged, or sample status?

8. Are the company's products or services on the wane? Are sales down markedly? Is the industry itself on the wane? How do company sales compare with its main competitors?

9. What are the past relationships between inventory and accounts receivable buildup, between sales, inventory and receivables buildup, between payables and inventory buildups? Have there been any material changes recently in these relationships?

Internal Risks and Threats: Security Environment

1. Review and inspect terrain and topography of the site, fencing, lighting, guardposts, parking areas, shipping, receiving, staging and storage areas, intrusion alarm systems, access and egress procedures, doors, locks, windows, surveillance equipment, and patrol methodology.

2. Review personnel policies, practices, procedures, and priorities with respect to employee honesty, such as management's philosophy toward its human resources, recruitment and selection standards, termination policies, development and promotion policies and practices.

3. Review information handling, classification and protection practices, policies, and procedures to determine their adequacy.

4. Review inventory and property accounting controls (raw materials, finished goods, parts, small tools, and portable equipment).

5. Review cash and securities handling practices, procedures and policies, authorizations, and other controls.

6. Review computing and communications systems to determine adequacy of physical security safeguards, disaster/recovery plans, information protection practices, and telecommunications security.

7. Review the past history of the firm with respect to critical incidents that have security implications, such as past thefts of property and proprietary information by employees.

External Threats and Risks

Determine:

- The current status of economic conditions for business in general
- The current status of competitive conditions in the specific industry of which the firm is a member
- The relationship between the firm and its competitors
- The long-term outlook for the firm's products and services
- The market share of the firm and whether that share is growing, constant, or declining

5

ESTABLISHING EFFECTIVE COMPLIANCE PROGRAMS

Compliance programs are usually created to meet requirements embodied in federal or state laws, regulations, or contract provisions. An effective compliance program can also serve as a framework for establishing internal controls and other safeguards designed to protect company assets.

A business or organization must also communicate to its customers, employees, shareholders, suppliers, the government, and the media that it is honest and ethical and that it complies with laws and regulations. Should things go wrong, if the business is suspected of or charged with a violation of law, one of its first and most valuable liability defenses is to show it had an effective compliance program in place prior to the offense.

Compliance programs are required at state and federal levels under a host of statutes. Here is just a sampling:

- The United States Sentencing Commission Guidelines for organizations requires that ethics policies, codes of conduct, and how to report misconduct be communicated to all employees.

- The Securities and Exchange Commission (SEC) requires stock brokerages to have compliance and supervision policies. These policies must be communicated to brokers in a way that is easy to understand, with clear examples of prohibited conduct.

- The Private Securities Litigation Reform Act calls for auditors to examine a publicly traded company's internal controls and assess the effectiveness of compliance programs.

- The Equal Employment Opportunity Commission requires that standards of fair, nondiscriminatory behavior be communicated to all employees.

- The American Law Institute has issued its Principles of Corporate Governance law standards that spell out director liability for inattention to corporate compliance systems.
- Under virtually every federal and state statute there are requirements "to promulgate and communicate" standards embedded in the law.

Is it worth the effort of a company to spend money and time on creating effective compliance programs and communications? Ask a company that has just lost a copyright or trademark infringement suit. Better yet, ask a company that just won a suit or escaped indictment. Ask how many hours of management time the suit ate up. How many hours did the attorney log? Avoiding even a charge of infringement is worth the effort.

A BUSINESS OWNER'S Q & A ON COMPLIANCE PROGRAMS

Q: Why does our organization need a compliance program?

A: The U.S. Sentencing Commission Guidelines have given a broad legal definition and a blueprint to an organization for the establishment of "an effective program to prevent and detect violations of law." Having an effective compliance program means that the organization has exercised due diligence. The organization must, however, take a number of concrete and workable actions to demonstrate due diligence. The carrot of due diligence can mean a reduction in fines (the stick) for organizations convicted of a violation of law.

Another reason for having a compliance program is the Guidelines' broad definition of *organizations* to include corporations, partnerships, associations, joint-stock companies, trusts, pension funds, unions, unincorporated organizations, and nonprofit organizations.

Companies using computers and communications systems have made it easier to violate a federal law. Some of the laws covered include: false claims, conspiracy, computer-related crime, fraud and deceit, bribery, extortion, money laundering, tax evasion, embezzlement and other forms of theft, insider trading, antitrust, and copyright or trademark infringement.

A BUSINESS OWNER'S Q & A ON COMPLIANCE PROGRAMS

Q: Are there any benefits from having a compliance program?

A: Yes. There are five specific financial and legal benefits:

1. Should your organization be charged and convicted of a criminal violation, having an effective compliance program could result in a lowering of fines or leniency in prosecution.

2. Lessening of directors' and officers' liability. In the September 1996 Caremark decision, the Delaware Chancery Court said effective compliance programs could shield directors from liability for the wrongful acts of company managers and employees.

3. Controlling legal costs. The requirements of a compliance program mean an organization must be aware of the possible legal risks associated with its business. In essence, this awareness is a form of preventive law that can reduce litigation costs.

4. Maintain and enhance corporate reputation. For many companies, especially those in consumer products, financial services, or healthcare, their reputation is their most valuable asset. Consumers often make purchasing decisions solely on the reputation of the company and its product or service.

5. We are in a global economy, and businesses may confront cultural and economic risks. A compliance program is the ideal vehicle for preparing employees on such topics as acceptable conduct in business contracts and payments, hiring and managing workers, and foreign laws and regulations. Being prepared means avoiding litigation risks that turn into shareholder suits, government prosecution, and bad publicity.

Q: Aren't all communications programs expensive?

A: Communicating compliance does not have to be expensive. To meet a standard of relevant, understandable, and measurable, company-specific compliance, information materials need to be focused and written in plain English. This information can be delivered in a variety of ways. Full-blown media programs with glossy brochures, newsletters, training films, or role-playing sessions are not always necessary.

Q: We already have a compliance manual. Isn't that enough?

A: Compliance manuals and other materials need to be evaluated periodically, both for possible new compliance risks and to test how well the material is understood by personnel.

AN OVERVIEW OF REQUIREMENTS FOR COMPLIANCE PROGRAMS

The U.S. Sentencing Guidelines contain a unique proposition. If organizations convicted of illegal acts prove they had an effective compliance program designed to detect and prevent criminal conduct, they could possibly get reduced sentences or fines.

The Sentencing Commission defines a compliance program that meets its standard of an effective program to prevent and detect violations of law as a "program that has been reasonably designed, implemented, and enforced so that it generally will be effective in preventing and detecting criminal conduct."[1] That a program may fail to detect a specific offense does not mean the program is ineffective. "The hallmark of an effective program to prevent and detect violations of law is that the organization exercised due diligence in seeking to prevent and detect criminal conduct by its employees and other agents."

The Commission describes "organizational due diligence" as including at least the following seven steps:

1. The organization must have established compliance standards and procedures to be followed by its employees and other agents that are reasonably capable of reducing the prospect of criminal conduct.

2. Specific individual(s) within high-level personnel of the organization must have been assigned overall responsibility to oversee compliance with such standards and procedures.

3. The organization must have used due care not to delegate substantial discretionary authority to individuals whom the organization knew, or should have known through the exercise of due diligence, had a propensity to engage in illegal activities.

---

[1] All quoted material in this chapter is taken from the U.S. Sentencing Guidelines.

4. The organization must have taken steps to communicate effectively its standards and procedures to all employees and other agents, by requiring participation in training programs or by disseminating publications that explain in a practical manner what is required.

5. The organization must have taken reasonable steps to achieve compliance with its standards. For example, utilizing monitoring and auditing systems reasonably designed to detect criminal conduct by its employees and other agents and by having in place and publicizing a reporting system whereby employees and other agents could report criminal conduct by others within the organization without fear of retribution would be reasonable steps.

6. The standards must have been consistently enforced through appropriate disciplinary mechanisms, including, as appropriate, discipline of individuals responsible for the failure to detect an offense. Adequate discipline of individuals responsible for an offense is a necessary component of enforcement; however, the form of discipline that will be appropriate will be case-specific.

7. After an offense has been detected, the organization must have taken all reasonable steps to respond appropriately to the offense and to prevent further similar offenses — including any necessary modifications to its program to prevent and detect violations of law.

COMPANY-SPECIFIC COMPLIANCE PROGRAMS

Compliance programs cannot be uniform; each company must develop its own and design it to be effective in preventing and detecting violations of law within the organization. Several factors can be used to develop a program:

- Size of the organization. How formal and elaborate a compliance program will depend on the size and complexity of the organization. A larger organization should have written policies describing prohibitions to specific acts and procedures to be followed by employees and agents.

- The likelihood that certain offenses may occur because of the nature of the organization's business. Where there is substantial risk that certain types of violations may occur, management must have taken steps to prevent and detect those types of offenses.

- Prior history of the organization. This should indicate the types of offenses the organization should take steps to prevent. "Recurrence of misconduct similar to that which an organization has previously committed casts doubt on whether it took all reasonable steps to prevent such misconduct."

SETTING UP AN EFFECTIVE COMPLIANCE PROGRAM

Organizational Due Diligence

The Sentencing Commission Guidelines call for the establishment of "an effective program to prevent and detect violations of law." Having an effective program means that the organization has exercised due diligence. The organization must, however, take a number of concrete and workable actions to demonstrate due diligence. In other words, a paper plan is insufficient, a program embodied in a manual is insufficient; a proactive, operating program is required. The following steps should be considered the minimum for an effective compliance program and used as an outline guide.

Ethics and Codes of Conduct

The Guidelines call for the organization to establish "compliance standards and procedures . . . reasonably capable of reducing the prospect of criminal conduct." This means written ethics policies and codes of conduct that discourage and deter unethical and illegal behavior. The codes should be distributed to management and employees and contain specific prohibitions.

Assigning Oversight

The compliance program must have "specific individual(s) within high-level personnel of the organization" in charge. The organization must have "used due care not to delegate substantial discretionary authority" to persons the organization knew or should have known "had a propensity to engage in illegal activities."

Responsibility for the integrity of an organization begins and ends with the chief executive or company owner. Only top management's attitude and support can create and maintain an effective overall control environment. Therefore, the person or persons in charge of the compliance program should be either the top officer or drawn from top management.

Communicating Compliance Requirements

A key element of an organization's compliance program is communicating, through a variety of ways, ethics policies and codes of conduct. How to carry out such a communications program is left up to the organization. The Commission said that communication should reach "all employees and other agents." This may be done by "requiring participation in training programs or by disseminating publications that explain in a practical manner what is required."

Internal Controls and Compliance Audits

The organization must take reasonable steps via monitoring and auditing systems that will detect criminal conduct by its employees and agents. The Guidelines imply that an organization should have accounting and systems controls to detect and deter waste, fraud, theft, and abuse of assets. Informal mechanisms related to organizational structure and management controls are also useful.

Reporting Systems

The Guidelines also require that the organization create and publicize a reporting system for reporting criminal conduct within the organization and that allows employees to do so without fear of retribution.

There are several ways to handle this requirement. A policy directive from corporate management should first clarify when to report criminal conduct, under what circumstances, and to whom.

A *hotline* is a mechanism that has been used in government and business. The major elements that have been found necessary for a successful hotline are:

- A clear statement of the hotline's mission and objectives
- Staff with interview skills and compliance program knowledge
- Controls to protect the confidentiality of callers
- Internal guidelines to evaluate and classify allegations received through calls or letters
- Policies that inquire into the allegations must be performed by independent and qualified personnel
- Case-monitoring procedures to assure they are being handled and resolved properly

Enforcement

Disciplinary mechanisms must be established for violations of law as well as for the failure to detect an offense. The "form of discipline that will be appropriate will be case-specific." Be careful: adequate discipline, obviously, can conflict with union rules and employment laws.

Investigative Responses

Once an offense has been discovered, though not fully verified, the organization must take all reasonable steps to respond appropriately to the offense.

This means the organization must start an internal investigation of the incident and it will be allowed a reasonable period of time to conduct it. An incident need not be reported to the appropriate governmental authorities if the organization reasonably concluded, based on the information then available, that no offense had been committed.

It may be possible to treat an incident of possible wrongdoing as a business problem—finding the guilty parties, satisfying insurance claim clauses, loss recovery, and strengthening of internal controls.

Every organization should have an internal investigation game plan. This means, first, a board of directors' resolution or a policy directive from management that clarifies and answers these questions:

- What misconduct (broadly defined and at what level) will trigger an internal investigation?
- To whom should the incident or misconduct be reported?
- When should an investigation be initiated?
- Who should conduct the internal investigation and under what circumstances?
- What should be the purpose of the investigation?
- What types of disclosures are mandatory?
- How do we create and maintain confidentiality and work-product protections?
- How can the corporation lessen the possibility of collateral prosecutions and sanctions?
- If the investigation leads to subcontractors, should they be considered agents?

Everyone involved in an internal investigation must be aware of the organization's policy and strategy on internal investigations, the laws that could have been violated by the organization or its personnel, and laws affecting the gathering of information and evidence.

SUMMARY

An effective compliance program must be driven from the top down. It must be motivated by top management's understanding of the dangers of liability for not having adequate internal preventive controls to protect company assets and by an awareness that a compliance program can offer possible benefits including limits on corporate liability and awards for punitive damages, and the positive public perception of being viewed as a strong and competent company.

The Sentencing Guidelines offer organizations flexibility in setting up a compliance program. This allows an organization to identify the acts it must prevent and focus its educational activities in those areas.

ESTABLISHING EFFECTIVE COMPLIANCE PROGRAMS

Finally, the compliance program must be active and ongoing; it can't be static. Policies, codes, controls, audits, investigations, enforcement, and responses must be monitored, reviewed, and updated in light of new legal developments and company experiences and the results of audits and investigations must be acted upon. Retraining will be necessary for the same reasons.

6

COMPUTERS AND ETHICS: AN OXYMORON?

The reasonable use of information technologies requires that all human links in the chain of use and development be properly and adequately informed of their rights and obligations.

The application of moral principles to a given host of actors and situations is what ethics is all about. Ethics teachers, however, like those in many other fields of study, are not all of one mind. There are at least three schools of thought in general and several schools of thought on information ethics in particular. The general schools of thought include utilitarian, contractarian, and pluralist philosophies.

The yardstick utilitarians apply is the notion that when facing moral dilemmas, the choice should be the one that gives the greatest good for the greatest number. In essence, a cost/benefit analysis is made and the social cost is compared with the social benefit.

The contractarian school reviews choices based on universal rules—human rights, fairness, and equity.

The pluralistic school would suggest that the choice should be predicated on the obligations we owe to one another based on our relationships—employer-employee, buyer-seller, etc.

In the field of information ethics, there are those authorities that argue that information is knowledge and should be made freely available to all because it liberates the mind. The opposing school holds that information is property to be owned for investment, held as a proprietary interest, rented, sold, or shared with selected others at the will of the owner.

Both ethics and justice essentially involve the determination of the rightness or wrongness of a human act in terms of its nature or short-term and long-term social, political, and economic consequences. In making an assessment of the rightness or wrongness of an act, therefore, practitioners of ethics and law consider a number of factors:

- The intentions at the time of the act. What did the instigator intend to gain and at whose expense?
- The act itself. Is the act, by its nature or essence, evil? Is it immoral, unconscionable, unfair, arbitrary, capricious, or unreasonable? Is it opposed to the natural law—the law of conscience? Or, was there a failure to act when duty required action?
- The pre-existing relationship of the parties. Does the relationship of the actor to the person acted upon impose any special added duties, obligations, or responsibilities on the actor toward the person acted upon? Does the special relationship require action instead of inaction under the circumstances?
- The short- and long-term consequences of the action or inaction on the primary parties involved. Who gained and how much? Who lost and how much? Who benefited most, and was it a fair allocation of benefits?
- The short- and long-term consequences of the action or inaction on society as a whole or on other parties of interest. What are the immediate societal consequences? What are the impacts on employees, shareholders, creditors, customers, clients, contractors, and suppliers? What are the impacts on future generations?

THE OBLIGATIONS OF COMPUTER-OWNERS AND COMPUTER-USERS

Computer-owners are responsible for the following:

- Providing standards and controls for data security, accuracy, integrity, and completeness
- Monitoring for exceptions to standards and controls
- Providing plans for contingencies
- Providing a safe and healthy work environment for users
- Education of users to treat and use computer resources responsibly
- Protection of confidential information from unauthorized access and disclosure
- Formulation, communication, and enforcement of standards that assure no such access or disclosures are made

Computer-users are responsible for:

- Complying with all safety, security, and internal control standards
- Using computer resources safely, securely, and for company purposes only
- Sharing computer resources equitably
- Accessing only those files, data, and programs over which one has authority
- Disclosing only that information one is authorized to show and only to a person who is authorized to receive it
- Protection, preservation, and proper maintenance of computer resources at one's disposal
- Refraining from conflicts of interest
- Refraining from theft or personal use of computer time, communications systems, or other corporate assets

THE STATE OF ETHICS IN THE WORKPLACE

New corporate-sponsored ethics programs appear to be making a meaningful difference in improving employees' attitudes about the behavior of their companies and influencing their responses to misconduct when it occurs.

The "Employee Survey on Ethics in American Business: Policies, Programs and Perceptions," conducted by the Ethics Resource Center in Washington, DC, questioned 4,035 U.S. workers in a cross section of small, medium, and large U.S. businesses. According to survey respondents, although misconduct in the workplace continues to be a serious problem, there is still strong reluctance to blow the whistle. The survey found that nearly one-third of all employees have witnessed some form of misconduct at their companies in the last year which they thought violated company policy or the law. Of those witnessing such misconduct, fewer than half reported it to their companies. The most common types of transgression observed by employees were: lying to supervisors (56 percent), lying on reports or falsifying records (41 percent), stealing and theft (35 percent), sexual harassment (35 percent), abusing drugs or alcohol (31 percent), and conflicts of interest (31 percent).

EFFECT OF ETHICS PROGRAMS

The survey also revealed that a growing percentage of companies now have formal ethics program in place. In particular, 60 percent have codes of ethics; 33 percent have training on proper business conduct; and 33 percent have an ethics office or ethics ombudsman to whom employees can go for advice or to report concerns about questionable business conduct. Twenty percent of employees reported that their companies employed all three procedures, defined as a "comprehensive program," including a code of conduct, employee ethics training, and an ethics office.

Comprehensive ethics programs appear to increase employee awareness of, and active response to, ethical and legal misconduct. Employees in companies with comprehensive ethics programs were more likely to have witnessed misconduct than those in companies with no programs, by a margin of 35 percent to 26 percent. Employees at firms with ethics programs also appear to be more sensitive to misconduct, evidenced by their classifying more types of behavior as sexual harassment and being more aware of conflicts of interest and violations of gift and entertainment policies.

Actual reporting of misconduct increases significantly for individuals in companies with ethics programs: 57 percent of employees with ethics programs reported the ethical and legal lapses they observed, compared to only 49 percent of employees whose firms had no such programs. Of those who did report misconduct, those with ethics programs were much more satisfied with employer response than those with no programs: 58 percent vs. 46 percent. While the majority of those with programs were "satisfied," the majority of those without programs were "dissatisfied" with their companies' responses.

In another noteworthy finding, employees who failed to report misconduct were much more likely to give as their reason for inaction "possible retribution or retaliation" from supervisors if they worked for a company without an ethics program (54 percent to 38 percent). Sixty-nine percent of employees at companies lacking an ethics program, compared to 57 percent with programs, believed that "corrective action would not be taken." Nonetheless, those with ethics programs were more likely to say that they did not want to be known as a whistleblower by a margin of 30 percent to 17 percent.

Ironically, those with programs were also nine percentage points more likely to say they sometimes feel pressure to cross the line to meet business objectives (33 percent vs. 24 percent), suggesting a heightened sensitivity to pressures for misconduct.

Ethics programs appear to make a real difference in employee perceptions of management. Employees with ethics programs, again contrasted to workers at companies with no ethics program, were considerably more likely to believe that the ethical commitment by their CEO (65 percent vs. 47 percent), senior management (70 percent vs. 52 percent) and direct supervisor (77 percent vs. 58 percent) was appropriate ("about right").

The impact of ethics programs on companies' treatment of stakeholder groups was also examined in the survey. Respondents at firms supporting ethics programs were much more likely to hold that their companies carried out their ethical obligations "exceptionally well" to:

- Customers (62 percent vs. 46 percent)
- Suppliers/vendors (36 percent vs. 29 percent)
- Distributors (33 percent vs. 22 percent)
- Public/community (54 percent vs. 31 percent)
- Stockholders/owners (45 percent vs. 31 percent)
- Government regulators (47 percent vs. 25 percent)
- Management (40 percent vs. 30 percent)
- Non-management employees (32 percent vs. 24 percent).

Other survey findings include:

- A code of conduct as the sole component of an ethics initiative seemed to produce employee attitudes and perceptions more negative than where nothing was done.
- In responses to five hypothetical questions regarding legal and ethical behavior, a higher percentage of respondents in organizations with no ethics programs responded that they did not know what was acceptable in the scenarios presented.
- The responses to the hypothetical questions on business law indicate that confidence in one's knowledge of the law increases

unjustifiably with rank in the organization. For example, senior managers were the least likely to respond that they did not know the correct answers, while hourly employees were much more likely to say they did not know. However, senior managers were, on the whole, no more or less likely than those at other levels to select clearly acceptable responses.

- In answering questions on basic business law, respondents in job functions to which certain areas of law related more than others (e.g., anti-trust and competitive intelligence for sales and marketing employees) tended to believe most actions were acceptable, including those actions which would be legally questionable.

- Generally, respondents at higher levels in the organization held more positive views on ethics. Conversely, respondents in lower ranks held more negative views on ethics. The greater reported pressures to engage in misconduct and the higher incidence of observed misconduct reported among mid- and lower-level employees suggest that senior management may be unaware of significant pressures felt by other employees and of much of the misconduct that occurs within their own organizations.

- Employees in technical positions seemed to be the most difficult to serve with ethics programs. Although this group was the most likely to report that their companies had codes, training, and ethics offices, they were the least likely to rely on these elements or to find them useful.

- Employees in administration, human resources, and public relations had the best perceptions of their companies' commitment to ethical business conduct and of their companies' unwillingness to ignore or encourage misconduct to achieve business objectives.

- The finance and insurance industries and the transportation, communications and public utility industries had the highest elements of a comprehensive ethics program.

- Dishonesty, in the form of lying to supervisors and lying on reports or falsifying records, was the most frequently witnessed type of misconduct in almost all industries.

ETHICAL ENVIRONMENT ASSESSMENT

Answer the following questions to gain understanding of your ethical environment.

1. Does management display a high sense of business ethics toward its varied audiences (i.e., shareholders, employees, vendors, competitors, and the communities in which it does business)?

2. Are company executives involved in community activities that enhance the arts, sciences, education, local economy, and the quality of social and political life?

3. Are the religious rights and freedoms of employees respected?

4. Are the rights of personal privacy of employees respected?

5. Is the information disseminated to shareholders honest, factual, and adequate to make intelligent and informed investment decisions?

6. Are the demands made on vendors reasonable?

7. Are competitive tactics by the firm fair and reasonable when compared with the industry?

8. Are employees treated as individuals?

9. Is sufficient time provided for employees to enjoy their families, communities, leisure, and personal or professional renewal?

10. Overall, what is the level of organizational ethics practices by the firm?

7

DESIGNING
PERSUASIVE
POLICIES

The Computer Security Institute's 1997 *Computer Crime and Security Survey* was composed of questions submitted by the FBI. The survey was sent to companies and government agencies and responses were received from 428 organizations. The survey reveals that even among companies that have some computer security, it may be inadequate in terms of policy, administration, and employee awareness and training.

Some of the survey findings include:

- Over 50 percent of the respondents didn't have a written policy on how to deal with network intrusions; 60 percent didn't have a policy for preserving evidence for criminal or civil proceedings; and 70 percent didn't have a "warning" banner stating that computing activities may be monitored.

- Over 20 percent of the respondents didn't know if they had been attacked. Less than 17 percent said they would advise law enforcement if they had been attacked. Over 70 percent cited fear of negative publicity as the primary reason for not reporting.

This report provides a policy framework and describes how policies can be a focus for defining core company values and goals, which then can be implemented through standards, guidelines, and performance indicators. Through policies, a company can assert its right to supervise and ensure an efficient and secure workplace.

The objective is to produce policies that provide clear, accurate, and persuasive communication on required conduct for employees. Policies are a means of educating employees on ethical and legal obligations that may, in turn, reduce potential litigation risks for the company. Policies also foster a company climate of recognizing an obligation to obey laws and of not tolerating acts that skirt or breach laws.

Finally, this focus on policy will allow a review of current company policies on information/communications systems use, privacy, and assets protection, and to save time, money, and frustration associated with developing a policy from scratch.

POLICIES FROM THE TOP DOWN

Organizations that have a Board of Directors or outside owners may produce Executive Limitations policies to ensure that the Chief Executive Officer (CEO) or manager carries out duties in a prudent and ethical manner.

For example, the Board may direct the CEO not to allow corporate assets to be unprotected or unnecessarily placed at risk. Intellectual property and proprietary information assets may be specifically cited along with physical and financial assets. The CEO might also be prohibited from endangering the company's public image or taking any action that is imprudent or unethical.

ETHICS AND CODES OF CONDUCT

At the next-lower levels, policies may further define unethical and imprudent behavior as well as specific assets to be protected. Policies should specifically forewarn employees of the consequences of prohibited acts. This means written ethics policies and codes of conduct that discourage and deter unethical and illegal behavior. The codes should be distributed to management and employees and they should contain specific prohibitions such as: abuse and misuse of computer systems, theft, embezzlement, fraud, destruction of company property, falsifying attendance, payroll, production and expense reports, gambling on company time and property, and sexual harassment.

Controlling unethical conduct in organizations is largely a matter of role modeling. If executives and supervisors behave ethically, employees tend to conform to an ethical standard. After role modeling, the next best defense is the establishment of a corporate code of ethics and an anti-crime policy. Written codes of conduct, adopted and adhered to by top management, can have a positive effect in deterring unlawful behavior in the organization. The establishment of the code isn't the end of the problem. The code must be enforced. Enforcement procedures should also be spelled out so that violations get reported, investigated, and disposed of.

In attempting to control and reduce abusive or criminal acts, management must communicate clearly to employees that such acts are considered to be and will be treated as serious problems. The major consequence of a policy is that it conveys to employees the organization's concern and unambiguously communicates that abuse of company property will invoke sanctions on the guilty employee.

DEVELOPING A POLICY

There are three main points to keep in mind when developing a policy:

1. The outline of any policy may be reviewed or entirely written by legal counsel. Certainly, the final draft should be reviewed and approved by the responsible company officer and counsel.

2. The policy should be reviewed periodically and updated in light of new legal developments and corporate experiences.

3. The policy is not an employment contract.

PROHIBITED CONDUCT

A clear statement forbidding specific illegal actions against and affecting fixed or liquid company assets should be included. Also, the policy should cover misuse of the company's computing and communications systems, other related systems, and equipment that could be used to carry out any illegal acts.

PROMULGATION OF THE POLICY

The policy can be communicated to employees through an employee handbook (maintain a log of employees who receive the handbook), a posting on employee bulletin boards, or through physical distribution of printed text. It is extremely important that the policy is written clearly, easily understood. The recipient should sign off, initial and date the copy of the policy.

Communications is at the core of an effective policy or code of conduct. Without it, a policy is meaningless, and worse, it will not pass legal scrutiny. A communications program must be ongoing, reflecting changes in a company's perceived risks, and responding to new legal and regulatory mandates. Communications must respond and follow these changes, and always maintain a strategy of testing and proving that the message is getting through to the personnel.

REPORTING SYSTEMS

The company should create and publicize a reporting system for reporting possible criminal conduct within the organization that allows employees to do so without fear of retribution. There are several ways to handle this requirement. A policy directive from corporate management should first clarify when to report a possible illegal act, under what circumstances, and to whom. Additionally, policy statements should state that suspected wrongdoing will be investigated thoroughly, and that suspects will be treated fairly and consistently without regard to position within the company or length of service.

INVESTIGATIVE RESPONSES

Once an offense has been discovered, though not fully verified, the company must take all reasonable steps to respond appropriately to the offense. This means the company must conduct an internal investigation of the incident and complete it within in a reasonable period of time. Responsibility for conducting an investigation should be stated: internal auditing, security, legal counsel, or outside investigators. An incident need not be reported to any appropriate governmental authorities if the company concludes, based on the information then available, that no criminal or compliance-related offense had been committed.

The company should have in place a systematic records and document retention and destruction program designed to be effective in meeting the legitimate business needs and legal obligations, including internal investigations, of the corporation.

If a criminal act is uncovered, the company will report to and cooperate with law enforcement; investigative results will also be reported to the audit committee. The company may report an incident to the bonding company as required under an insurance policy.

ENFORCEMENT AND SANCTIONS

The following seven traits should apply to enforcement and sanctions:

1. They should be consistent in application.

2. Disciplinary mechanisms should exist for illegal conduct, unethical conduct, and failure to detect an offense.

3. Definition of the conduct that is grounds for termination should be clear.

4. Disciplinary measures should not conflict with employment or federal labor laws or union rules.

5. Disciplinary measures will apply to supervisors, managers, and executives who condone questionable, improper, or illegal conduct by those reporting to them or who fail to take appropriate corrective action when such matters are brought to their attention.

6. Termination action should not conflict with the personnel manual; the policy should spell out precisely what the company would do to an employee harming or misusing equipment or stealing company property; consult with legal counsel on termination action.

7. The legal department shall report periodically each confirmed violation of this policy of which it has knowledge to management and the audit committee.

If the company policy on illegal behavior has an immediate termination/no exception clause, the company had better be prepared to defend it. While such a clause may be consistent, most companies prefer a two- or three-stage procedure, moving into a disciplinary policy of warning, counseling/reminder of the policy, and then termination or prosecution.

An alternative clause could say: "Violation of corporate policies by employees will invoke disciplinary measures up to and including termination."

Company policy concerning prosecution should always be clearly stated and be in the name of the Chief Executive Officer. The prosecution policy should include a requirement that anticipated actions be reviewed with legal counsel prior to their initiation.

AUDITS OF POLICY COMPLIANCE

The purpose of auditing is to monitor compliance with policy directives and procedures. These audits should include:

- Set frequency and timing
- Supervision by internal audit department
- Focus on formal and informal management controls and assessment of effectiveness
- Thorough review of all controls in each area
- Documentation and reporting findings to the audit committee of the Board of Directors

QUESTIONS TO ANSWER ABOUT YOUR POLICIES

As a review, imagine that you are in court or arbitration with an employee charged with and dismissed for theft. How would you answer the following 14 questions posed by the judge or arbitrator?

1. Does your business have a policy covering employee theft?

2. Was such a policy organization-wide?

3. Did the policy cover all employees?

4. Did top management issue the policy?

5. Was the policy developed because the organization had past experience of serious losses due to employee theft and pilferage?

QUESTIONS TO ANSWER ABOUT YOUR POLICIES

6. If the business has had serious losses, could they be substantiated with internal audit or security reports or insurance claims?

7. Did the policy, or company rules, state a dollar value threshold for items stolen?

8. Did the policy spell out precisely what the company would do to an employee stealing company property?

9. Did the company anti-theft policy have an immediate termination/no exceptions clause, or a two- or three-stage procedure, moving into a disciplinary policy of warning, counseling/reminder of the policy, and then termination or prosecution?

10. Was company policy concerning prosecution clearly stated and in the name of the Chief Executive Officer?

11. Did the company's prosecution policy include a requirement that anticipated actions be reviewed with legal counsel prior to their initiation?

12. Did the employee know the anti-theft policy rules and did the employee acknowledge this?

13. Was the company's anti-theft policies inserted in the employee handbook and did employees do a one-time sign-off on the entire handbook? Were company rules and policies clearly and repeatedly communicated to employees?

14. Is the company consistent in applying those rules?

8

COMMUNICATIONS SYSTEMS POLICY GUIDE

E-mail is considered to be analogous to an internal memo, a private postal system, a letter or postcard, a telephone, a cell phone, a publication, a bulletin board for tacking up messages, or the Worldwide Web with near instantaneous broadcasting capabilities. An E-mail system can have all these characteristics plus user convenience, informality, and spontaneity.

At times, however, some E-mail users send messages that are demeaning, abusive, discriminatory, or simply "untouched by human thought." Lawyers love to find these uncensored messages on E-mail systems—they refer to them as *hot documents* because such potentially incriminating statements can provide an opening to possible liability and litigation.

Operationally, E-mail systems provide not only message transmission, but may have a time/date stamp, a record of who received the message and when, and a logging and tracking of messages through a company and between companies or individuals. There may also be a record of the message distribution list as well as automatic archiving of messages. In short, a system may comprise a complete audit trail of who is sending what to whom and a road map to finding incriminating statements, or tracing a decision-making process to determine accountability.

An employer is vicariously liable for the tortious acts of an employee who is acting within the scope of his or her employment. This may include "acts" committed via E-mail. An emerging legal concept is the tort of negligent supervision, or failing to supervise an offending employee. Organizations are faced with both lessened standards of liability and mandates to report possible regulatory, civil, or criminal misconduct of its employees or even by the organization itself.

The main employee misuses of communications systems include: excessive personal use of the system; use for an outside business;

personal investing, gambling, or accessing pornography; infringing intellectual property rights; and sending malicious and harmful messages.

This chapter is designed to be a guide for employers, managers, supervisors, and employees on how to avoid language and acts via the company's communications system (E-mail, pagers, cell phones, and the Internet, etc.) that could infer defamation, discrimination, harassment, invasion of privacy, negligence, or other liability against individuals, the organization, or its agents.

Throughout this chapter, the focus will be on E-mail. However, many of the problems discussed and solutions proposed could also apply to other elements of a communications system, such as bulletin boards and websites. These systems may also transmit information to the public, thus affecting the potential liability exposure of the organization. Drafting an E-mail/communications systems policy plus sample policies on system use and electronic evidence are included in this chapter.

COMMUNICATIONS SYSTEM POLICY CONSIDERATIONS

To control and limit the misuse of its E-mail and other elements of its communications system, an organization must develop a policy and set of procedures that cover:

- Network and E-mail systems, computer hardware and software, and connections to online services and other networks
- The ownership of the communications systems and purposes for which it is to be used
- Fair, nondiscriminatory treatment of all employees
- E-mail and other electronic messages that are obscene, offensive, or project discrimination, harassment, or any form of abuse
- Enforcement and penalties for misuse
- A preventive law awareness program for communications system users

The company must deal with the presence of a discrete expectation of privacy with respect to E-mail and other elements of the communications system. The organization should promulgate a clear statement on communications system privacy designed to eliminate an employee expectation of privacy and assert employer ownership, authority, and oversight of the communications system. Employee usage of the communications system is at the employer's discretion. The employee uses the communications system with rules and restrictions that are designed to protect the employer's property and serve legitimate business interests, such as the employer's need to identify messages that might compromise the employer's legal interests.

Policies, rules, and actions should clarify that individual access to the communications system is via key or password and is administered by security or network administrators. The network may be monitored and message contents filtered (a software filter program can block some obscene, racist, and sexual material) and system-generated files may be searched and seized at any time and for any reason.

The Electronic Communications Privacy Act's (ECPA) prohibitions on communications system monitoring and disclosure exempt business uses, specifically allowing:

> "An officer, employee, or agent of a provider of wire or electronic communication service, whose facilities are used in the transmission of a wire communication, to intercept, disclose, or use that communication in the normal course of his employment while engaged in any activity which is a necessary incident to the rendition of his service or to the protection of the rights or property of the provider of that service."

Another clause of the ECPA allows interception of communications if the "electronic device" used for interception is:

> "any telephone or telegraph instrument, equipment or facility, or component thereof, furnished to the subscriber or user in the ordinary course of business and being used by the subscriber or user in the ordinary course of its business or furnished by such subscriber or user for connection to the facilities of such services and used in the ordinary course of its business."

Presumably, monitoring and filtering software would meet the definition of "component thereof."

The ECPA only covers the interception of electronic communications transmitted via common carrier.

The outline of any policy may be reviewed or entirely written by legal counsel. Certainly, the final draft should be reviewed and approved by the responsible company officer and counsel.

SAMPLE COMMUNICATIONS SYSTEM POLICY OUTLINE AND CONTENT

External and internal corporate electronic communications system covered:

- Microcomputers, terminals, and networks
- Messages, drafts, records, documents, and other information on the communications system including backup media and storage

Statement of content:

- The corporation's communications system sole purpose is to assist in conducting the business of the enterprise.
- All computers and communications equipment and facilities, including E-mail, and the data and information stored on them are to remain at all times business property of the corporation and are to be used for business purposes only.
- It is the goal of the corporation to maintain a work environment for all its employees that is absent disparate treatment and will not tolerate abuse or discrimination against candidates or existing employees.
- The corporation's communications system may not contain messages having language or images that may be reasonably considered offensive, demeaning, or disruptive to any employee, or creates a discriminatorily hostile or abusive work environment. Such communications system message content would include, but would not be limited to: sexually explicit comments or images, gender-specific comments, racial epithets and slurs, or any comments or images that would offend someone based on their race, color, sex, religion, national origin, age, physical or mental disability, status as a veteran, or sexual orientation.
- The corporation reserves the right to monitor all communications system message content.

- Any views expressed by individual employees in communications system messages are not necessarily those of the corporation.
- The corporation shall establish a systematic communications system message, records and document retention and destruction program designed to be effective in meeting the legitimate business needs and legal obligations of the corporation.
- Violation of corporate policies by employees will invoke disciplinary measures up to and including termination.
- This policy will be reviewed periodically and updated in light of new legal developments and corporate experiences.

E-MAIL EVIDENCE

Electronic mail and some other electronic communications (pagers, cell phones) have become a valuable source of evidence in lawsuits.

Evidence Recovery

Another critical point about E-mail: data and messages supposedly erased from a hard drive or magnetic backup media may be restored by various data recovery/forensic methods. Magnetic media is normally re-writable; deletion, in DOS, erases the pointers on the file and leaves the information in the disk's clusters. To erase data, a file cleaning program or disk re-formatting is usually necessary.

Message Encryption and Privacy

Selection of an encryption device will provide only a reasonable measure of message privacy. Encryption does not mean that the message has been erased after sending; encrypted data is no different than other data written to disk.

E-mail Evidence Policy Considerations

To control and limit the disclosure of E-mail information, corporations and other organizations must develop a policy and set of procedures that cover:

- The purposes for which E-mail is to be used

- Enforcement and penalties for misuse
- Purging of E-mail files
- An E-mail records retention program
- The legal consequences of destruction or loss of E-mail evidence
- A preventive law awareness program for E-mail users

E-MAIL EVIDENCE POLICY CHECKLIST

Policy Statement

The corporation shall establish a systematic E-mail message, records and document retention and destruction program designed to be effective in meeting the legitimate business needs and legal obligations of the corporation.

Policy Implementation and Procedures

To cover external and internal corporate E-mail and other elements in the communications system such as:

- Computers, terminals, and networks
- Messages, drafts, records, documents, and other information on the E-mail system including backup media and storage

Determine relevance of all material on the E-mail system that is:

- Vital to corporate operations
- Potential legal or regulatory importance
- Required by law or regulation to be part of document retention program
- Material that can be purged in the course of business operations (cost controls, expense reductions, lack of storage space, etc.)

Materials to be retained or purged, and on what schedule, will be determined by advice from:

- Legal counsel
- Records Management Director
- Division manager, department head, or group supervisor

SAMPLE E-MAIL EVIDENCE POLICY CHECKLIST

- Chief Financial Officer or Controller
- Chief Information Officer or MIS Director

Material to be retained should be:

- Sorted, indexed, and stored according to records retention requirements
- Vital operational material to be handled by department manager, financial officer, or Chief Information Officer

Material to be purged should be permanently erased or otherwise destroyed, including any copies or backups. Conditions under which purging of E-mail materials should cease:

- Upon receipt of notice of imminent legal action, receipt of subpoena, discovery motion, indictment, or other legal notice
- Suspension notification from legal counsel
- The suspension of any corporate document or computer file purging program, including possible litigation-related E-mail that could possibly involve discoverable material
- Depending on the discovery request, an organized search for E-mail material will be conducted
- All E-mail material collected will be screened for response to discovery and for privilege protection
- E-mail material will be identified and marked, indexed and duplicated.

Retention and destruction program may resume on notification of legal counsel or on compliance and lifting of discovery motion or cessation of litigation.

SAMPLE E-MAIL EVIDENCE POLICY CONTENT

This policy of the corporation is to cover the entire and internal corporate E-mail system, including: computers, terminals and networks, messages, drafts, records, documents, and other information on the E-mail system including backup media and storage.

The corporation's E-mail system sole purpose is to assist in conducting the business of the enterprise.

COMMUNICATIONS SYSTEMS POLICY GUIDE

All computers and communications equipment and facilities, including E-mail, and the data and information stored on them are and remain at all times business property of the corporation and are to be used for business purposes only.

The corporation devises and maintains the security of its computing and communications systems as well as the monitoring of such systems, including E-mail. The use of all passwords and other identification and verification security devices must be made known to the corporation.

The corporation reserves the right to monitor all E-mail message content.

Any views expressed by individual employees in E-mail messages are not necessarily those of the corporation.

The corporation shall establish a systematic E-mail message, records and document retention and destruction program designed to be effective in meeting the legitimate business needs and legal obligations of the corporation.

Violation of corporate policies by employees will invoke disciplinary measures up to and including termination.

This policy will be reviewed periodically and updated in light of new legal developments and corporate experiences.

9

INTERNAL PROTECTION CONTROLS

There should be a common understanding among management, auditors, security and computer personnel, and legal counsel that:

- Management is responsible for establishing internal controls that assure the security and integrity of computer and communications, as well as accurate reporting of financial information regarding their organization and the effectiveness of its internal control systems.
- The function of the auditor is to examine and attest to the accuracy of the financial information and to examine internal controls that safeguard assets from loss.
- There are internal controls that apply to all companies and there are internal controls that cover all assets—financial, physical, and intellectual.

MANAGEMENT CONTROLS

Establishing effective and efficient management controls tends to be a matter of balancing costs against benefits. Tipping the balance to either extreme (overcontrol or undercontrol) is inefficient and ineffective. The cost of implementing controls is far easier to calculate than the intended benefits of such controls because costs tend to be quantitative while benefits tend to be qualitative. Deciding how much control should be exercised in any organization is not a simple matter. Both economic and behavioral considerations include direct and consequential costs (acquisition, implementation, and maintenance costs).

Behavioral considerations have to do with the impact controls may have on personal productivity. Do control costs impact on human performance and job satisfaction? Worse yet, do controls take on the aura of absolute rules, prohibitions, and mandatory actions and thus discourage judgment and discretion? Slavish compliance is required when controls are designed and enforced without rationality, without need, and without consideration for the sensitivities of the people they affect. They become more venerated in their violation than by their compliance. Covert and overt resistance can follow. In fact, in some organizational settings, overcontrol often results in petty acts of fraud and thievery (i.e., lying on expense accounts and fudging performance data, as methods of rebellion).

PRINCIPLES OF COMPUTER CONTROLS

A *control* is any device, action, or procedure that reduces the likelihood of an exposure to the risk of asset loss. Almost all fraud and embezzlements have occurred because specific controls were compromised, either intentionally or accidentally, or because management ignored their warning.

For example, validity checks are designed to:

- Separate duties, as between those with property-handling responsibilities and those with property-recording responsibilities.
- Determine that (a) a purchase has been approved by someone with authority to commit funds for such purposes, (b) a purchase is from a vendor who is approved, (c) a purchase is by a person who is authorized to buy, (d) that specific goods ordered were in fact received, and (e) that the unit price charged and extensions are stated correctly on the vendor's invoice.
- Provide an oversight mechanism at each step in processing a transaction to detect errors, omissions, and improprieties in the previous step. This can be accomplished through division of labor and dual responsibility for related transactions (i.e., counter-signature, segregation of functions, dollar authorization limits, etc.). The oversight mechanism should force collusion by at least two parties to effect a fraudulent transaction.

Validity checks involve authorization procedures established to determine whether a payment to be made is based on a legitimate claim against the company by a vendor or supplier who has in fact supplied something of corresponding value.

SECURITY VULNERABILITIES AND CONTROL ISSUES

Employee Screening Policies

Conduct background inquiries on employee applicants on:

- *Criminal records.* Use public records to obtain criminal histories.
- *Driving records.* If the applicant may be using a company car, obtain a driving record from the state motor vehicle department.
- *Past employment references.* Employers should attempt to contact past employers and document information. The applicant should be asked for four to five people he or she reported to at each of the last four or five positions.
- *Education and credential verification.* Contact educational institutions named by the applicant, or state licensing boards.
- *Credit standing.* It may be necessary to use an outside agency to stay in compliance with the Fair Credit Reporting Act.
- *Pre-employment assessments,* specifically personality assessments that provide an indication of the characteristics a person displays over time, such as trustworthiness or emotional stability.
- *Attitudinal assessments.* These provide an indication of a person's attitudes about work-related issues, such as honesty.
- *Pre-employment structured interviews.* These are designed to go into more depth, based on information from the above sources, to help further develop the applicant's profile.

Basic Financial Controls for the Professional Office or Small Business

Remember that anyone is capable of committing embezzlement or fraud. Establish, monitor and enforce the following internal controls:

- Bookkeeper, office manager or accountant, and key personnel are secured with a fidelity bond.
- Separate duties—no one person should control an entire financial transaction.
- All blank checks and signature stamps are physically secured.
- Only the owner or senior officer should sign company checks.

- Verify all documents in any transaction of goods or money before signing.
- Monitor cash receipts (that the cash deposited reflects the actual cash intake).
- Total invoices, check the amount posted, and reconcile with the amount deposited.
- Have bank statements sent to your (owner's) home or delivered by courier only to you.
- Reconcile bank statements—match bank statements with deposit slips and checks; check the amount, payee, and signature on each check.

Physical Security Issues

- Security of check stock, signature stamps, and check imprinting equipment.
- Secure storage locations for cash, securities, bonds, and other financial instruments.
- Encoding of company checks with information on operator, date of printing, and serial number.
- Physical security features in checks: watermarks, security inks, chemical voids, reflective holograms, high-resolution microprinting, void pantographs, bar coding, glyphs, and perforators.
- Secure storage for removable files and fonts.
- A daily list of checks written on the account provided by the bank; this is matched by bank and verified by customer.

Controls and Security

- Accounting, bookkeeping, and key personnel are secured with a fidelity bond.
- All blank checks and signature stamps are physically secured.
- All cash, securities, and other financial instruments are stored in a physically secured area or safe or vault.
- All blank invoices, purchase order forms, and credit memos are physically secured.
- The purchasing department is separated from receiving responsibilities; the supervisor is not authorized to pay bills.

- Approval for payment is given only when the related purchase order and receiving copy is attached.
- The purchasing department uses pre-numbered orders for all purchases; copies go to receiving and accounting.
- Two persons supervise cash or credit returns.
- The purchasing department is periodically audited.
- The person who prepared the payroll does not sign payroll checks
- The amounts paid are confirmed with the payroll records.
- Signature endorsements on cashed checks are compared with signatures on employment records.
- Work orders, rates paid for overtime, temporary or part-time help are reviewed frequently.
- All canceled and unclaimed checks are accounted for and secured.
- The computer operator/bookkeeper does not handle cash, open incoming mail, mail statements, do follow-ups on delinquent receivables, approve write-offs of bad accounts, or approve refunds or credits.
- The cutoff bank statement is used to audit the cash account; this is done periodically and on a surprise basis.
- Bank reconciliations performed, reviewed, and verified each month.
- Blank checks are never signed.
- Checks are never signed without supporting documentation (purchase orders, payroll forms, invoices).

ACCOUNTING INFORMATION ACCESS CONTROL PROCEDURES

Accounting program controls should be able to:

- Restrict users to specific directories, programs, menu choices, and data files.
- Deny permission to copy specific documents, to transfer data onto disks, or to send out restricted information via E-mail or other electronic transfer.
- Create authorization tables that can limit user access to read-only, data input, data modification, and data deletion capabilities.

INTERNAL PROTECTION CONTROLS

The accounting software should also provide information/file masking, change-detection, audit trails; intrusion detection/alarm; recovery from network or database crashes; multi-level user rights for menus, forms, queries, and reports; file encryption; and database logs.

Accounting software should be evaluated for security in terms of how well it can enforce a segregation of duties that will deny or flag situations like unauthorized changes to finance charges, check formatting, invoices and statements, job costing, shipping and billing documentation, or sick time and vacation accruals.

ELECTRONIC COMMERCE CONTROL ISSUES

- Lack of authentication of transaction authorization.
- Interception of data by outsiders.
- Lack of physical access control to computer system.
- Inadequate and weak access control system.
- Introduction of computer viruses to networked systems.
- Inadequate control over storage media.
- Single user in a microcomputer system authorizes and records transactions.
- Check management software that specifies limits to dollar amounts of signatures.
- Management awareness and support of computer security measures is low or absent.
- Users have the ability to enter a range of specific database choices.
- Sensitive fields are available on data entry screens.
- Users may download accounting information to personal computers.
- Critical computer file backup procedures are not enforced.
- Multilevel password control systems are not in use.
- Password-controlled disk lock system is not used.
- Networks are not protected by any type of firewall—screening routers, operating or application-based system.
- Cryptography is not used in either computer communications or storage systems.

10

SECURITY— FROM FENCE TO FIREWALL AND BEYOND

Total, absolute security is impossible; you can't secure everything, nor can you foresee every possible threat. Security and other preventive controls can provide only reasonable, not absolute, protection against cybercrime.

Security strategy can be to protect the weakest links in systems. Our choice is that of a value-based model. Simply put, the most important assets get the most protection. This means considering which assets, if destroyed or stolen, would cause the greatest financial, operational, or reputational loss, damage or liability.

Physical security and access control are taking on greater importance in deterring cybercrime by establishing barriers that must be overcome to reach a target and enforcing separation of duties and providing audit trails. Knowing the basics of physical and computer access control will help you understand how these systems operate from building entry to communications networks.

PHYSICAL SECURITY: AREAS AND EQUIPMENT

A physical security survey of the areas to be protected often starts with a blueprint, layout, or drawing of the area to be surveyed and marking entry points and types of existing doors, closures, and locks. Note any security or fire equipment already in place. This drawing can be used to analyze placement of access control units and, perhaps, tie in any security, safety, and fire detection equipment for monitoring on one system.

Note also the traffic flow and patterns in the area during both normal working hours and off hours.

ACCESS CONTROL

Access control is a process by which an individual is challenged, and if verified, is then allowed access to a specific facility or interior area or object, such as a computer, or its software applications, or to communications networks. The basis of access control is identifying a person seeking access.

Methods of identification usually include something a person has (a key, a card, a token), something a person knows (a password, a code), something a person is (a personal characteristic or physical attribute such as fingerprints), or something a person does (a signature or a computer keystroke pattern).

Levels of Control

There are three general levels of access control. In the lowest level, there are locks and keys, code/combination locks, passwords, badges, etc. Advantages of these items are that they are usually inexpensive, easy to use, have employee acceptance, and require little training and judgment by security personnel. Disadvantages include not providing positive identification/verification of authorized holder; item or knowledge needed for access can be lost, stolen, or disclosed; or the item may be counterfeited.

At the next level, there are various ID cards, photo badges, personal recognition by a guard or other authorized person, and combinations or two-level systems requiring a coded card and cipher or digital/keypad entry system, for example. The advantages of these systems are that it is only moderately expensive and compromise of the system is more difficult, as two items of identification are required. Magnetic stripe cards are part of an established, low-cost, secure, reliable, efficient, and worldwide-accepted system. Advances in magnetic stripe technology have allowed a number of combinations, such as digitized personal biometric attributes. Disadvantages of these systems are that counterfeiting or impersonation is possible and reliance on judgment of security personnel may be too great.

Non-repetitive systems, one-time passwords, and the use of random passcode generation with a keypad or hand-held decoders offer increased security in that there is no pattern to the authentication that can be copied.

At the highest level, there are the biometric systems, which have the following advantages: It is very difficult and costly to forge or counterfeit an individual's unique physical characteristics; and the deterrent effect is very high. Disadvantages include costs that are higher than the costs for most other security devices; enrollment and access times may be higher than for other systems.

Passwords

Passwords are the most common form of computer access control. A password can be very simple—a single letter or number; or complex—an algorithm based on date or time. A password can be chosen by the computer user or assigned to the user. User-chosen passwords are usually "weak," that is, easy to guess or reveal through a dictionary or password-cracking software. A drawback to assigned passwords is that they are often too difficult to remember and people then tend to write them down so they won't forget them.

PASSWORD SECURITY CHECKLIST

❑ There should be written policy and procedures on selecting and disclosing passwords.

❑ Passwords should be kept secret and known only to the user.

❑ Passwords should not be displayed near or on the user's computer.

❑ Passwords should be difficult to guess and easy to remember; they should have a minimum length and alpha and numeric characters.

❑ System-assigned/generated passwords are usually preferred.

❑ Passwords should be encrypted when kept in the computer system.

❑ Passwords should be changed regularly, monthly, every 60 days, or three months if user-selected. Six months is an option for system-generated passwords, but no longer than once a year for any password.

❑ Passwords and other access codes should be deactivated immediately when an employee leaves the company.

❑ A periodic audit should be performed to determine if the company's password security policies and procedures are being followed and are still effective.

BIOMETRIC SECURITY SYSTEMS

Biometrics in security is the machine/computer identification and verification of persons based on biological or physiological measurements. In general operation, the system consists of a device that scans or replicates the characteristic to be measured. That is, the device may record a series of words, photograph or laser scan a fingerprint or an eye's vessel pattern. It might measure the length of a person's fingers and the spread of the hand; the speed, pressure, and size of a person's signature; or the speed and rhythm of keystrokes in data entry. The computer and appropriate software store, process, and analyze the measurements.

For securing access to a computer, a database, or a network, a system based on positive identification of the user would be desirable. A positive ID system would provide an accurate and legally convincing audit trail for financial/information transactions or for investigations of computer-related fraud.

The major biometric security systems in use today and how they operate are described below.

- *Facial scanning.* Also called facial thermogram or mapping, facial scanning relies on an algorithm for pattern recognition unique to an individual's face. For access control, a small video camera is connected to a computer. The person seeking access looks into the camera and the scanning verifies or rejects the person depending on the scanning match. In a computer terminal access application, a camera can continuously view the terminal users and confirm their identity. If the authorized person leaves or another sits down at the terminal, the security system's facial recognition algorithm can trigger a sign-off by the original terminal user and require the new user to sign on before using the terminal.

- *Fingerprints.* A computerized system uses electro-optical recognition and file matching of fingerprint minutiae.

- *Fingertips.* Algorithms are derived from measurements of the individual's fingertip shape and texture.

- *Hand geometry.* An electronic scan of a person's hand is made first. Ninety different aspects of the hand are measured and compared to a previous scan of the person which provided a reference profile. This encoded profile data is stored either in computer memory or on a magnetic stripe or in a smart card (see next section). A positive match between the current hand scan and stored data allows access.

- *Iris recognition.* The iris is the colored ring around the pupil of the eye. A scanning device measures and analyzes the unique color patterns of the iris and takes a video picture of the iris, which is converted into a digital code that can be compared.

- *Keystroke dynamics.* This system measures the speed and pattern of keystroke entry of an individual.

- *Retinal patterns.* This system recognizes an individual by the retinal vessel pattern of the eye. A scanned reference picture is stored in a computer as a standard for comparison and matching.

- *Signature dynamics.* Automated signature verification systems are based on the dynamics of the signer's pen motion related to time. The measurements are signature shape, speed, stroke, pen pressure, and timing, taken via a digitized tablet. A signer is enrolled by taking three or more measurements of his signature; an average figure is obtained and stored in the computer. Future signatures are compared with the average figure.

- *Voice verification.* "Prints" of a person's voice are recorded in analog signal which is converted to digital and a set of measurements are derived and stored in a computer. The references are based on an individual's vocal pattern by speaking several single words. The system may require an individual to say three words out of a reference file of seven, a match of the words spoken with those on file allows access.

SMART CARDS AND PORTABLE DATA CARRIERS

A smart card functions as a portable database, a computer in a package the size of a credit card. Its most common form is that of a standard credit card, but it can also be configured like a personal identification badge or any other shape required. The card allows information to be accessed and retrieved via a card reader. Software resides within the reader and is also located on the card in the form of integrated circuits. The function of the reader is to detect the presence of a card and to provide a standard interface so that the card can communicate with different hosts.

Security can be built in, such as a multiple-level, hierarchical structure guarded by a password and/or personal identification number (PIN), bar code, or a biometric ID. Smart cards are multi-technology devices providing access control IDs for computer and database access, digital and cellular communications, and authentication and encryption, as well as decryption keys. Smart cards are carrying chips with faster processors and bigger read-only memories. They are becoming easier to use with smaller or radio frequency readers.

SELECTING AN ACCESS CONTROL SYSTEM

For the most part, today's biometric systems are compatible and integrate with access control systems that may be card-based. Therefore, when considering a biometric system, you should examine your current access control system and what you want to accomplish by adding or integrating a biometric system. Let's start with a review of basic system selection guidelines.

Some basic questions you will have to ask vendors are:

- How stable or reliable is the biometric attribute itself?
- What can affect it? Include the percentage of the population that lack the attribute, those who have no fingers, can't speak, have glaucoma, etc.
- How accurate is the measurement of the biometric?
- What is the system's storage capacity for biometric data?
- What is the throughput or operating speed of the system?
- What is the average enrollment time for users?
- Is the system really needed? Is it too technical, too intrusive, too invasive; is there a possible liability in making and storing biological details of a person? What further "evidence" can be gleaned from biometric data?
- How easy is it for the system to be "layered" with another biometric or ID?

The vendor should also supply information on error rates for false rejection, false rejection of authorized personnel, false acceptance, and the admission of an imposter. For high security, a very low false acceptance rate is important. Where authorized personnel should be allowed access with a minimum of inconvenience, a low false rejection rate is desirable.

SECURITY SURVEYS

Physical Security

Here are some questions you should ask when considering physical security:

- Is there an access control and physical security system?
- Is the system totally functional?
- Are personal computers, lap-and-palmtops, and notebooks secured with an alarm system, lock-down bars, cables, chains, fasteners, or other physical security devices?
- Are disk drives secured with key locks?

Data Processing Areas/Rooms/Equipment

This term includes mainframe, PCs, network servers, or data media storage. Consider the following questions:

- What hours do the computer areas operate?
- How many days per week?
- Are employees who are authorized to enter data processing areas required to use a company-issued personal identification device? Is positive ID required for all vendors or consultants entering the computer or communications areas?
- Are all other employees prohibited from freely entering computer areas?
- Are signs posted on all entry doors prohibiting all non-authorized persons from entering? Is there a security log for visitors and employees?
- Are guards or data processing supervisors positioned to observe any unauthorized entrant?

- Under what conditions, if any, are non-authorized persons given access to data processing areas? Are they then under constant observation?
- Is an access log kept of all persons who enter the data processing area?
- Are storage media disks marked with a company logo or other identifiers?
- Is company storage media leaving the facility subject to search and examination, including contents?

DATA BACKUP AND SECURITY

Physical security for data media and storage areas is not only common sense, but for some organizations such as banks, it may be a legal mandate. For instance, the Office of the Comptroller of the Currency, in Banking Circular 229 on Information Security, states:

> "Controls must exist to minimize the vulnerability of all information [particularly that which is produced, stored, and transmitted by computer] and to provide necessary security. The level of control must be assessed against the degree of exposure and the impact of loss to the institution. This includes dollar loss, competitive disadvantage, damaged reputation, improper disclosure, lawsuit, or regulatory sanctions."

> Security should be designed to: "prevent unauthorized alteration during data creation, transfer, and storage; restrict physical access; and maintain backup and recovery capability."

- Is sensitive/vital software and documentation secure (payroll records, personnel records, accounts receivable information, etc.)?
- Is a back-up file kept at a secondary site? If yes, are there any controls?
- Do data back-up and records retention and maintenance follow either laws or company policy?
- Is there a thorough, appropriate, and tested disaster recovery plan?
- Are re-start procedures fully documented?

SECURING THE WEBSITE

Website security restricts access to the internal Web server and to a mainframe, to an intranet, the Internet, or the World Wide Web. Another area of security concern are transactions between the Website and suppliers or customers. Internal security consists of access controls and firewalls. A firewall is simply a configuration of security access control, filtering, and screening technology designed to keep out unauthorized traffic from an unsecured and untrusted network. Communications and transaction security often means the use of encryption and digital signature technologies.

An overview of website security should include the following questions:

- Has company policy defined the authorized traffic and access into and from the website?
- Is the security of your Internet connections adequate?
- Is there access control technology or a complete firewall system for the Web server and other computing and communications equipment with online connections?
- Does the communications/transaction system have the ability to authenticate customer and client information?
- Does the website provider have a comprehensive security policy that is communicated to its employees? Is this policy enforced?
- Are the employees trained to be competent in security procedures and technology?
- Are all security measures monitored and audited?
- Can you answer "yes" to the above questions for your operation?
- What will the Internet or website provider do if service is interrupted?

ELECTRONIC PAYMENTS AND SECURITY TRANSACTION SCHEMES

Commercial electronic transactions are attempting to secure customer financial information several ways. One is to take the customer's financial information off-line, encrypt it, and never display it live on the Web. The most common encryption method is the Data Encryption Standard (DES); another is public key encryption. Other software applications may use a Graphics User Interface (GUI) keypad, employing proprietary algorithms that randomly encrypt numbers, for example on a credit card, and send the numbers one at a time.

NETWORK ACCESS CONTROL

Generally, network security has been designed to keep unauthorized users from accessing the network, either externally or internally. The main technique has been a firewall, a security control gateway that channels communications and information.

A firewall seeks to control access to legitimate network users who have different authorization levels to applications and resources. For example, a firewall may insulate part of a network, such as a server, perhaps, containing accounting and financial data.

SECURITY AND LIABILITY RISKS

Years ago business was conducted directly between buyers and seller on a face-to-face basis. Technology has replaced the old forms of contact and many firms do business via computer and communications systems, usually called electronic commerce. One of the forms of buying and selling is Electronic Data Interchange, or EDI.

Until recently, if a company wanted to take advantage of EDI, the setup required an expensive investment in hardware and software. Today, small businesses can take advantage of a VAN(value-added network) or Internet-based EDI. The Internet allows companies to exchange ordering, shipping, payment, and inventory information. A VAN is usually offered by a large company to smaller companies without full EDI capabilities. However, Web/Internet-based EDI is becoming the vehicle of choice for most small businesses. Another Internet option is a virtual private network (VPN), a collection of technologies that provide secure "tunnels" over Internet lines. A VPN can provide site-to-site connectivity and security features such as firewalls, compression, encryption, authentication, and public key exchanges. VPN technologies are available for Windows NT and UNIX.

Basically, EDI is the automated exchange of structured business data, such as invoices, purchase orders, and other documents and forms, via computer between businesses. If payment information is exchanged—credit or debit instructions—through the banking systems' automated clearing houses or certain VANs, then it is financial EDI. Usually these are separate exchanges of financial and nonfinancial data, depending on networks, VANs, and banks.

An EDI type of information exchange is based primarily on contract; a set of promises, for which if broken, there is a legal remedy. This means that trading partner agreements can include descriptions of forms and documents, payment terms, delivery schedules, as well as specific control, security, and audit measures. The American Bar Association has a "Model Trading Partner Agreement" which defines terms of an acceptance and allows for adoption by parties of electronic signatures ("symbols or codes which are to be affixed to or contained in each document transmitted by such party"), encryption, and other security measures.

All contracts for the sale of goods over $500 come under the Uniform Commercial Code (U.C.C.) Section 2-201, the Statute of Frauds. This section requires the contract to be in writing and signed by the party. To meet the requirements of 2-201, the writing must evidence a contract for the sale of goods, be signed in a way that authenticates and identifies the party to be charged, and must specify the quantity. A complete signature to authenticate a writing is not necessary. "Authentication may be printed, stamped, or written; it may be by initials or by thumbprint. It may be on any part of the document and in appropriate cases may be found in a billhead or letterhead."[1]

DIGITAL SIGNATURES AND SECURE TRANSACTIONS

Federal legislation has been introduced on the use of digital signatures. Utah, Florida, Wisconsin, California, and other states already have laws. A broad legislative definition of a digital signature is to be found in California's Digital Signature Act. A digital signature is defined as an electronic identifier, created by a computer, and intended by the party using it to have the same force and effect as the use of a manual signature. While addressing transactions in state government only, the Act defines any written communication in which a signature is required or used, "any party to the communication may affix a signature by use of a digital signature that complies

---

[1] U.C.C. Section 2-201.

with the requirements of this section [of the Act]. The use of a digital signature shall have the same force and effect as the use of a manual signature if and only if it embodies all of the following attributes:

- It is unique to the person using it.
- It is capable of verification.
- It is under the sole control of the person using it.
- It is linked to data in such a manner that if the data are changed, the digital signature is invalidated.
- It conforms to regulations adopted by the Secretary of State [of California]."

As in funds transfers, security measures can support the legal enforcement of contracts and agreements by ensuring the authentication and integrity of the communication. However, courts will look at the claimed and to-be-proven effectiveness of security techniques and equipment, as is the case with security under U.C.C. 4A, which covers commercial electronic funds transfers.

RECORDKEEPING FOR EDI

EDI recordkeeping, backup, storage, and recoverability should follow those described for other electronic records. The purpose is to ensure EDI records will provide legal proof of transactions should a legal dispute arise. Another reason is to satisfy government records requirements. In EDI, gauging when to capture and store data is critical, but it is often system or transaction-specific. One should also consider keeping a complete trade data log of all transfers sent and received. The goal is getting the most accurate reproduction of an original record that can be made; in short, for business and legal purposes, a reliable and provable final-form record that will be in a secured electronic repository.

SECURITY AND RISKS IN EDI

EDI presents some risks that are significantly different from a stand-alone computer or a dedicated system. Once outside access is permitted, the host system security should have a risk assessment. The basic concerns here are threats such as data system destruction and

damage, data disclosure and modification, processing delays, and denial of service. Backup and recovery should receive critical scrutiny.

To maximize its cost-reduction capabilities, EDI creates many databases, accessible by many people for many purposes. Typical access control features for individual EDI users include: terminal and user IDs, user behavior characteristics and normal patterns of use, and user authorization limits. These control measures are intended to restrict access to those persons with pre-established needs and to limit even those persons to data that are vital to the proper discharge of their job-related duties. The controls are intended to monitor, flag, and log exceptions and security rules.

DOWNSTREAM LIABILITY

Downstream liability could attach to a company where an outside hacker or an employee used the company's computer to attack the computer systems of trading partners or customers.

Risks	Remedies
Service interruption	Backup and recovery planning
Transmission interception	Cryptography
Electronic intrusion	Data access and authorization controls
Forced entry	Physical access controls
Data disclosure	Information classification/ dissemination controls
Data modification	Data accuracy/exceptions reporting controls
Embezzlement	Separation of duties and audit trails
Employee sabotage	Rewarding work environment
Insider/outsider collusion	No exceptions to access/ authorizations controls

11

PROTECTION OF PROPRIETARY INFORMATION

TRADE SECRETS

Information permeates an enterprise; it is often elusive, defying a flow chart or attempts at mapping its locations. Proprietary information is less slippery, having an importance attached to it by management. Intellectual property has legal status and thus a higher recognition. But not all important information, having value, is necessarily given this recognition at its birth. Much of it is in a state of becoming, not yet given status of a proprietary or an intellectual property niche. When information reaches a stage where it is seen as having value or potential value as an intangible asset that can contribute to the enterprise's earning power, then it deserves protection.

Trade secrets are information that becomes wrapped in concepts of value and protection as well as secrecy. The essence of a trade secret is that it has value; its ultimate value occurs when it finds the highest and best use, yielding the greatest return through exploitation either within the enterprise, or by transferring rights to others via licensing and royalty arrangements. Assigning a final value to trade secret information may be impossible given the many, often subtle, permutations of valuation. One thing is sure: an unused trade secret could be called worthless.

Before it can be exploitable, trade secret information is in its own stage of becoming; the potential is visible, but the package isn't ready. At this stage, however, the element of protection must enter, along with some recordkeeping, bookkeeping, and legal matters. Recordkeeping must start with identifying the information to be protected, retaining all the related documentation during development, and making sure all documents are signed and dated. Bookkeeping should not only be a record of costs (time, effort, and expense) of information development, but of the costs of protection as well. All records should be created and maintained to meet the business records standard under the rules of evidence.

The protection and value of trade secret information are joined in a series of cost-benefit analyses. This fact implies the use of periodic, focused audits of trade secret programs to monitor development, value, and protection compliance.

To understand trade secrets, we must first look at the relevant statutes and case law.

HOW TRADE SECRETS CAN LOSE THEIR CONFIDENTIALITY

Proper means to discover a trade secret include:

- Independent invention
- Reverse engineering
- Observation of the item in public use or on public display
- Obtaining the information from public literature

The clearest way to abandon secrecy is to make public disclosure of the information. This does not necessarily mean broad public dissemination; a single third party will suffice as long as the disclosure is made in the absence of confidential circumstances. A patent issuance will end trade secret status. The age or relevance of the information can also affect its trade secret status.

SECRECY AND PROTECTION

With trade secrets, we find the critical interdependence of law and protection. In asserting trade secret ownership, one has the burden of establishing that adequate safeguards to protect secrecy have been taken. Measures that have met previous legal tests of safeguards include employment agreements and practices of nondisclosure, vendor contracts, and the range of stringent security practices common in protecting classified information.

There must not only be sufficient security measures in place to insure secrecy, the information owner should be prepared to provide detailed evidence that the security was "reasonably sufficient under the circumstances," should a trade secret issue land in court.

Security measures normally could include:

- Hiring and discharge policies and practices, preemployment clearance
- Secrecy agreements
- Need to know rules, compartmentalized use/documents with clearly marked security classifications covering hierarchies of secrecy (confidential, proprietary, trade secret, etc.)
- Document handling procedures, logging, storage, declassification, archiving, and destruction
- Risk and vulnerability analyses, physical security policies, procedures, measures, equipment and systems, and administration; access control covering visitors, vendors, and employees
- Trade secret/security awareness programs
- Audits of all legal, administrative, security, training, and awareness programs related to trade secret protection; also regular limited-scope compliance audits
- Prepublication clearance for articles and information dissemination
- Enforcement and sanctions for violations of any security measures or disclosure of trade secrets

The legal interpretation of the phrase "reasonable under the circumstances," with regard to safeguarding trade secrets has varied in the courts. In several cases, the courts have held that security need only consist of reasonable efforts. In a 1970 case, *E.I. duPont de Nemours & Co. v. Christopher*, the court ruled that:

> "We should not require a person or corporation to take unreasonable precautions to prevent another from doing that which he ought not to do in the first place. Reasonable precautions against predatory eyes we may require, but an impenetrable fortress is an unreasonable requirement."

SECRECY AGREEMENTS

A secrecy agreement is a way for a company to keep its technical or business information confidential. A secrecy agreement is an agreement which creates a confidential relationship with either an employee or someone outside the company, such as a supplier or subcontractor. It is used for preserving secrecy with respect to inventions, technical information, know-how, and other information which may qualify as trade secrets.

A trade secret or confidentiality clause should be part of agreements with employees, independent contractors, consultants, visitors, vendors, distributors, lenders, partners, and shareholders.

A signed secrecy agreement is usually necessary to create or preserve intellectual property protection rights. Secrecy agreements should not be entered into casually and without legal advice or assistance.

While there is a common-law duty on employees not to disclose or use their current or former employer's trade secrets, and a fiduciary duty for officers, a signed agreement is evidence of an employer's action to protect trade secrets.

ELEMENTS OF A SECRECY AGREEMENT

Secrecy agreements should cover:

- The employee you want to enter into an agreement.
- The departments or subunits of the company involved.
- Where the agreement is likely to be performed (i.e., in which state of the United States?).
- A definition of trade secrets and the trade secret information the employee has access to. Indicate the particular product(s) or manufacturing process to which the information relates, as well as the kind of information, such as, software, designs, complete sets of manufacturing drawings, quality assurance reports, marketing studies or data, test specifications, process details, etc.
- When the information is to be available to the employee. If it will be available over a period of time, like the length of a contract or project, give the period of time.
- The fact that the company is protecting its trade secret information.
- That the employee will not disclose or misappropriate trade secret information.
- That the employee will report any unauthorized disclosure or use of trade secret information.

- The period of time the employee is to keep the information in confidence. Again, be specific. There should be notice of post-employment non-disclosure. This may be a separate agreement in the form of a restrictive covenant, which is a provision reasonably restricting (not too broad as to time, territory, or activity) competition by the employee after employment is finished. As the enforcement of restrictive covenants varies with states that permit them, they must be carefully drawn to conform to a state's law.
- If an employee takes action against misappropriation and injunctive relief is sought, set an agreed amount of bond or security to protect the employee against whom the injunction may be issued.

POINTS TO REMEMBER
ABOUT SECRECY AGREEMENTS

The following are important points to remember regarding secrecy agreements:

- Secrecy agreements must be reasonable in scope and not contrary to public policy.
- Only top management should be authorized to enter into and sign secrecy agreements with others.
- Secrecy agreements are enforceable, and injunctions may be granted and large damages awarded for not adhering to them.
- Avoid disclosing trade secret information to any outsider except under an enforceable secrecy agreement.
- Consult with legal counsel before entering into any and all secrecy agreements.

TRADE SECRET CONCLUSIONS

Regarding trade secret information, keep in mind the following:

- Keep records of the time and investment to create trade secret information.
- Identify by name and position all persons to whom trade secret information was disclosed.

- Use risk and vulnerability analyses to determine the threat of loss of trade secret information.
- Implement physical security measures that are obvious, reasonable, and adequate.
- Keep records of the costs of protection.
- Document and periodically audit all protective measures.
- Remember that trade secret protection is an ongoing program of cost/benefit analysis; protection should be adequate to threat and value.
- Confidentiality/secrecy agreements should be specific in terms of individual, information, location, and time/duration; a company-wide trade secret statement will likely be inadequate.
- Proprietary confidential information is seldom static; technology and service product life cycles have shrunk, often to less than two years. Protective measures must be as dynamic as the confidential information.

COPYRIGHT AND SOFTWARE COPYING

Unauthorized copying of software by employees can lead to charges of breach of contract or criminal copyright infringement. There is risk of liability for the organization and its officers and managers for not having software copying policies, for inadequate monitoring of licensed vendor software, as well as for failing to promote among employees recognition that unapproved copying of software is unethical and illegal.

COPYING AND DISTRIBUTION VIA COMPUTER

In-house copying and computer distribution of newsletters and other published materials violates the copyright law. The electronic storage of copyrighted material in a company database and sharing it with personnel via E-mail could easily jeopardize the entire network. A company found guilty of criminal copyright infringement—copying and distribution—could find "all . . . equipment used in the manufacture of . . . infringing copies"[1] seized and

---

[1] The Copyright Act of 1976, U.S.C. Title 17 §10.

destroyed by order of the court. Be aware that some publishers are offering bounties to employees or other insiders who provide details on illegal copying.

COPYRIGHT INFRINGEMENT: INDIVIDUAL AND ORGANIZATIONAL LIABILITY

Unauthorized copying of vendor software can lead to charges of criminal copyright infringement. When organizations purchase software, they are obtaining a license agreement that grants them a non-exclusive right to use the software. Copying software beyond the bounds of the license agreement could find the organization guilty of breach of contract or copyright infringement.

"Shrinkwrap" licenses, contracts on the box or inside which are found when the consumer removes the plastic wrap on a software package, have been upheld under state law contract principles. Such state law contracts, when enforced, are not preempted by federal copyright law. Netwrap and screenwrap agreements must give the customer a chance to opt out without risk of infringement liability.

Liability for Inadequate Protection

Organizations can be held liable for inadequate protection of copyright material if there is evidence that:

- The infringement was similar to a previous violation committed by the company and its employees (this could mean a failure to supervise).
- The organization did not take all economically feasible steps to provide a reasonable level of protection (copying policies, security, monitoring, and audits).

SOFTWARE USE AUDITING AND METERING

Tracking software in your organization that you are licensed to use, or checking to see that employees have not installed pirated software, has been made easier by utilities that can monitor users, computers, and files. This software can administer access to licensed software, report on usage, and verify that license agreements are not being breached. These metering products can also help control the costs of software usage by determining needs based on actual usage.

LESSENING AN ORGANIZATION'S LIABILITY RISK

An organization's basic legal defense strategy against criminal copyright infringement should include written software copying policies and codes of conduct that discourage and deter unethical and illegal behavior.

Since criminal copyright infringement comes under the U.S. Sentencing Commission Guidelines (Section 2B5.3), a wise choice for organizations is to follow the Sentencing Commission guidelines for compliance programs as described in Chapter Eight of the Federal Sentencing Guidelines Manual.

SAMPLE SOFTWARE COPYING POLICY CONTENT

This policy of the Corporation is to cover the entire and internal corporate licensed software usage, including microcomputers, terminals and networks. The Corporation's use of licensed software sole purpose is to assist in conducting the business of the enterprise. Licensed software is to be considered "business property" and is to be used for business purposes only.

All computers and communications equipment and facilities and the data and information stored on them are and remain at all times business property of the Corporation and are to be used for business purposes only.

The Corporation devises and maintains the security of its computing and communications systems as well as the monitoring of such systems, including licensed software. The use of all licensed software must be made known to the Corporation.

The Corporation reserves the right to assign usage of licensed software in any manner and to monitor all software usage.

PROMULGATION OF THE SOFTWARE COPYING POLICY

Each part of the software copying policy should be explained in detail:

- Define the nature of the license and contract and why it is important to the organization.
- Explain the copyright law and the possible sanctions employees, officers, and the organization could face for infringement or breach of contract.
- Desirable and undesirable behavior should be explained, described, and examples of each given.
- The annual software copying compliance audit should be described and reasons given for its necessity. Also explain any ancillary benefits of the audit, such as possible cost savings.
- Describe and explain unannounced audits.
- Explain the need for centralized control of software purchases, installations, and use monitoring.
- Describe how an employee can report unauthorized software copying and retain confidentiality.
- Detail the sanctions for unauthorized software copying.

POINTS TO COUNTER FALLACIES

Employees often harbor a number of misconceptions about copyright and the use of copyrighted material. In addition to explaining the software copying policy, it is a good idea to try to remove misconceptions. Here are a few remedies:

- Innocent copyright infringement is still infringement.
- If a work does not display a copyright notice, that does not mean the work is not copyrighted.
- Although federal registration is not required to have a valid copyright, registration is necessary for federal court jurisdiction and for obtaining statutory damages.
- A work displayed on the Internet does not mean the author has abandoned it.

- If you use copyrighted material, get permissions at each stage of the project.
- Not charging for a copy of a copyrighted work is still a violation of copyright law.
- Do not use any name or likeness of a celebrity without their permission; use without permission is a violation of their "right of personality."
- Photos or pictures of paintings and other artwork may be in public domain but the gallery, museum, or archive may own the right of access; you may need permission or a license to use the photo or a copy of the artwork.

MONITORING AND AUDITING

The organization must take reasonable steps via monitoring and auditing systems that will detect criminal conduct by its employees and agents. The organization should use annual and unannounced software copying audits that would detect and deter possible infringement, in addition to informal mechanisms related to organizational structure and management controls, including centralized administration of software purchases and usage. In decentralized companies, branches and subsidiaries would need similar controls and audits.

12

SETTING UP YOUR WEBSITE: BUSINESS, SECURITY, AND LIABILITY CONSIDERATIONS

12

SETTING UP YOUR WEBSITE: BUSINESS, SECURITY, AND LIABILITY CONSIDERATIONS

Below are general questions and statements designed to put the job of setting up and managing a website in a broad perspective. Many technical points have been left out. Too often, website creation begins and ends in a technical exercise. Most websites are a form of business communication and marketing. Technical considerations are vital, of course, but at the outset and throughout, the basic objective of the site should control every consideration from graphic design, intellectual property protections, to overall security.

WEBSITE PLANNING GUIDELINES

Given the range of possible website configurations, the variety of duties that must be performed, and the diverse sizes and resources among organizations, it is impossible to develop a model plan that would fit the needs of all organizations.

We can, however, provide a framework for developing a website plan and cover the basic liability and protection-related policies and decisions that must be addressed by an organization's management.

MANAGEMENT ACTIONS: POLICIES

Policies should be established to assist those responsible for creating and managing the website. Major policy decisions may require the input of top management as to the goal and objective of the website. A firm but flexible policy for the daily operations of the website must be established and supplemented by supportive policy to cope with any incident or emergency that might arise.

An administrative policy should clarify such questions as:

- Which department should have the overall management authority for the website?
- Who is the manager authorized to implement and administer the website?
- Who has the authority to make changes to the website?
- Who will be responsible for website compliance, security, and emergencies?

NAMING WEBSITES: DOMAIN NAMES

A domain name distinguishes a commercial site on the Internet by providing a unique name and address. Under an agreement with the U.S. Commerce Department, the governing body is now Internet Corporation for Assigned Names and Numbers (Icann). Domain names can still be registered with and administered by Network Solutions, Inc. (NSI) under its InterNic information center.

On the far right of a domain name is a standard abbreviation representing the type of entity, such as ".com" for commercial, ".edu" for educational institutions, and ".gov" for government entities. To the left of the type of entity is a unique domain name; left of this is the user name.

A domain name may function as a trademark and suggest identity, quality, and content of the Internet or website.

NSI acts only as a registrant of a domain name, on a first come/first served basis, and does not do any regular trademark searches to see if a trademark or trade name competes or can be confused with another. It is up to the applicant to assure that the domain name it registers does not conflict with another. In a dispute the applicant must prove the name was registered with the U.S. Patent and Trademark Office.

WEBSITE DESIGN AND INTELLECTUAL PROPERTY

Setting up a website and designing a Web page for your organization can involve the use of programmers and graphic or audiovisual designers. Often this work is outsourced.

WEBSITE DESIGN AND INTELLECTUAL PROPERTY

The individuals working on the website and page may not be familiar with the mix and requirements of intellectual property laws. It is a safe idea to assume these individuals do not know key elements of copyright and trademark law. Going on this assumption, below is a brief review of copyright and trademark basics, plus reminders of common fallacies held regarding specific areas of the laws.

Intellectual Property Laws

Intellectual property generally refers to ideas and information residing in various formats that is given the legal status and protection of property as an asset of an individual or enterprise.

Patents, trademarks, and copyrights are the three primary forms of intellectual property rights in worldwide use. They encourage the introduction of innovative products and creative works to the public by guaranteeing their originators a limited exclusive right, usually for a specified period of time, to whatever economic reward the market may provide for their creations.

A full discussion of intellectual property law is given in the Legal Reference section in this book.

Stealing the Best Ideas

In designing websites, it is often heard that it's okay to steal ideas that work. While this may not lead to a copyright infringement, it could result in a charge of plagiarism. Plagiarism is unfair use, defined in law as appropriating the literary composition (book, article, advertising copy and design, etc.) or the ideas or language and passing them off as the product of one's own mind.

Web Page Frame-Ups

Framing is a Web browser feature that lets a site put up an on-screen border, usually consisting of the framer's logo, advertising, and menu that remains when the user goes to various pages and can even stay on the screen when the user goes to another site.

WEB MARKETING: DEFAMATION AND FALSE ADVERTISING LIABILITY RISKS

Wrongful or negligent disclosure of private or embarrassing facts usually requires such information be communicated to more than one person. Any disclosure of false information could lead to a defamation suit. Defamation has two types of communication: defamation via print, writing, pictures, or signs is called *libel*; and *slander*, which is defamation by speech. Both are communications of false information to a third party that injures a person's or a business's reputation—causing bad opinion, public hatred, ridicule, or disgrace.

Other elements of defamation include the reasonable identification of the defamed person and damage to reputation. If the defamation refers to a public figure or is a matter of public concern, the plaintiff must prove that the defamatory language was false, and that it was communicated knowingly or with a reckless disregard to the truth or falsity of the information. The element of falsity, in speech of public concern cases, requires the plaintiff to prove it by either the standard of preponderance of the evidence, or most often, the more difficult clear and convincing evidence.

The basic defenses to defamation are that the facts of the statement are provably true and a privilege can be invoked. Absolute privilege is reserved for government officials, such as judges and legislators, and the content of most public records. The press has a qualified or limited privilege to report on matters of public interest that might go unreported. This qualified privilege can be lost if the information is in error and malice can be shown.

Under the common law of defamation, the defendant has the burden to prove truth as a defense. In a civil case, the standard of proof is normally a preponderance of the evidence, requiring the trier of fact or jury to believe that the existence of a fact is more probable than its nonexistence.

COMMERCIAL DEFAMATION

For commercial defamation, the statement or representation (commercial speech) must: have a tangible harm on the business; be made to a non-privileged third party; and be made by a party who was negligent in determining if the statement was false and defamatory.

WHO IS A PUBLISHER?

False statements by a competitor about another's products in advertising or promotion may come under the Lanham Act (15 USC Section 43(a)). In this section of the Act, the Federal Trade Commission (FTC) is charged with preventing and punishing unfair methods of competition or unfair and deceptive acts or practices in or affecting commerce. The Act covers false and misleading statements made about commercial products, via ads or promotions, that are believed likely to cause damage to the plaintiff's business. False disparagement of a competitor or competitor's goods is an unfair method of competition.

The FTC has the power to prohibit unfair practices and does so by first issuing a complaint of its charges to the defendant and ordering a hearing. The defendant can show cause why the FTC should not issue a cease and desist order. After testimony, such an order may be issued. Violation of the order by failing to stop the unfair practice could lead to a civil penalty of $10,000 for each violation. Cease and desist orders and liability can run to stockholders, directors and officers, employees, and agents.

WHO IS A PUBLISHER?

A critical problem for bulletin board operators, website owners or providers, and E-mail system owners is the definition of publisher or re-publisher vs. distributor or common carrier. A defamatory statement is published or disclosed to a third party directly or indirectly. With E-mail, a bulletin board, or a website, "broadcast" might be a better term.

Who is charged with publication, or as being a publisher, hinges on the amount of editorial control exercised over the communication. Editorial control means an element of knowledge, knowledge that the material was defamatory and therefore should not be published.

But how can true editorial control be exercised in a situation where a high volume of messages is speedily disseminated? Public bulletin boards, websites, and E-mail service providers argue that there is no way they can police all this digital traffic. Corporate websites and E-mail systems will have a harder argument because of lower volume and, in theory, more control over how their systems are used.

For corporations, broad disclaimers on message content are one way to lower potential liability. Someone has to have the responsibility of reasonable care for policing a system, for taking action when a problem such as defamation or copyright infringement occurs. Either service providers or some form of self-policing organization will have to:

- Handle reports of alleged abuses
- Develop software that will identify postings and trace the source
- Make an immediate investigation of the allegation
- Take action, such as deleting the offensive message
- Provide software that screens for defamatory messages or words prior to dissemination over the network
- Settle disputes, such as through an alternative dispute resolution method
- Publish retractions

WEBSITE PRIVACY PRINCIPLES AND POLICY

Websites have great potential for raising privacy liability risks. A conflict is almost inevitable as is marketing its products or services is a key reason for a business to have a website. A main reason for a person to visit a particular website is to examine its marketing information. When marketer and consumer meet, the dynamics of information exchange occur and privacy problems may take shape.

The website business usually desires as much information on a current or potential customer as is possible to obtain. The website business may obtain information openly—by asking—or surreptitiously, through the use of techniques that use the information residing on the customer's computer.

Website owners need to be aware of potential privacy problems that can cause legal liabilities and very bad publicity. For example, consider the methods of gathering information on site visitors. One popular device is the use of a "cookie," a browser feature that allows information to be read off or written to a computer's hard drive, such as which websites people visited and what they did at the site.

Cookies are a way for website providers to obtain and store information about their users, and to use that information for various marketing purposes. Since users often do not know about this method of information gathering, privacy issues may be raised. Recently, some updates to browser software allow the cookie to be disarmed, which seems to solve this particular privacy issue.

The customer, of course, may give information to the website business freely and without caring what the business does with it. Or, before giving out personal, marketing-relevant information, the customer may want something in exchange, and may want to know exactly how this personal information is going to be used. The information exchange dynamic has now added privacy concerns. The trick for the website business is to turn these privacy concerns into a business plus, rather than a minus.

Handling privacy concerns effectively may also have a long-run benefit for all website owners—it may hold off more restrictive laws and government regulations on how business can be conducted on the Web.

WEBSITE PRIVACY PRINCIPLES AND STANDARDS

The Open Profiling Standard (OPS) provides a voluntary framework covering the collection and sharing of personal information supplied by consumers visiting sites on the Web while assuring their privacy.

The Web user gets a common electronic form for listing personal information, such as marital status, home ownership, hobbies, and other relevant marketing-related information. Users are notified when a website requests personal information, then the user can give the site some or all of their personal information. The website must obtain the user's consent to give any personal information to another business or site.

The Platform for Privacy Preferences (P3) is a broader standard than OPS and would create a common set of computer codes that would allow a website to transmit its privacy policies to a user's browser software. Users can then use their browsers to communicate with websites that met the user's criteria for privacy. Currently, sites often use the browser feature cookies that can be read from or written to a user's hard drive. Data collection software routines, and these cookie files stored on a user's computer, can reveal the names of websites recently visited and activities during a visit, such as a transaction.

The World-Wide Web Consortium (W3C), which has a 170-company membership, put together the P3 privacy initiative and has the same goal as the Open Profiling Standard. W3C members Netscape and Microsoft will have browsers that will support P3.

TRUSTe, a non-profit group backed by Netscape, IBM, and AT&T, proposes a sort of licensing and branding/logo system (*trustmarks*) for website owners that will inform consumers of the website's privacy policies and practices, and provide an audit of those practices. Trustmarks would appear as icon buttons on licensed websites. A website would tell users how information about them would be used. When no personally identifiable information is collected, the type of trustmark is a *no exchange* trustmark. When personal information collected is only used by the company/owner, this is called a *one-to-one exchange*. When personal information gathered is sold to marketers or other third parties only with the consumer's consent, this is called a *third-party exchange* trustmark. This would mean that the user/consumer has a choice of giving the website any personal information.

A major accounting firm would do TRUSTe's audits of licensed websites. TRUSTe's contracting, licensing, and logos will be backed by court actions if necessary.

WEBSITE PRIVACY ASSESSMENT CHECKLIST

❑ Does your site collect personal information from site visitors through cookie files or electronic registration forms?

❑ How does your site use a visitor's personal information?

❑ What kinds of information are collected about site visitors?

❑ How will this information be used, and is there a user consent form covering company and third-party use of the information?

❑ Can visitors opt in or out of your marketing database or mailing list?

❑ Is the information current and accurate for its intended use?

❑ Can visitors look at, change, or delete any collected personal information?

WEBSITE PRIVACY ASSESSMENT CHECKLIST

❑ Do you describe the kinds of legal actions that would force the release of personal information to a third party?

❑ Does your site have a visitor's personal information privacy policy?

❑ Is your privacy policy posted or information disclosure notice posted on your website?

❑ Are your information privacy practices audited by an independent third party, such as an accounting firm, and are the results of the audit available to the website user?

13

DISASTER PLANNING FOR INFORMATION SYSTEMS

Most organizations would probably suffer a critical or total loss of function within two weeks if they lost their computer and communications support. Many companies couldn't survive a system or network outage that lasts 48 hours.

In addition to lost income, a disaster could cause a business to lose market share, business opportunities, customer satisfaction, market credibility, company image, brand value, or relationships with suppliers, creditors, and employees.

Failure to develop and implement disaster recovery planning for data processing operations and communications systems can also have negative legal consequences for a company and its owner and/or its directors and officers.

Management should recognize the essential procedures of a disaster recovery plan:

- Identification of critical information
- Recovery of critical information
- Designation of alternate sites (if necessary)
- Plan testing and evaluation

BUSINESS PLANNING vs. DISASTER PLANNING

Business planning tends to be strategic and proactive while disaster planning tends to be tactical and reactive. Since the disaster planner (who may also be the business owner) must deal with a host of contingencies and be ready to respond at a moment's notice when disaster strikes, the disaster planner needs to be constantly vigilant; there will be no advance warning system.

Disaster recovery plans (also called contingency, continuity, or resumption planning) can also be formulated via software. These programs should be examined carefully for flexibility to meet specific company needs plus vendor support and maintenance fees.

Natural disasters are generally the most uncertain events with which the disaster planner must contend—when a natural disaster will occur and its potential cost consequences. Here, the effort should be directed at answering questions like how quickly one can respond to minimize the loss? How and where do we operate in the interim?

Both natural disasters and acts of man such as hardware/software failures, inadvertent errors, sabotage, and mischief can disrupt computer operations and communications networks. Any number of hardware or software glitches can cause a system-wide disruption—and they are becoming more frequent with the increasing complexity and size of networks.

Many companies depend on data-processing capabilities to such an extent that even short-term delays in processing time create substantial financial losses and long-term delays can spell company ruin. The character of some unfavorable events can be truly catastrophic, like a wipe-out of accounts receivable or order processing systems where no duplicate files are maintained and where data can't be quickly reconstructed on a manual basis.

EQUIPMENT BACKUP

Being prepared for equipment failure or destroyed disks will make the recovery back to normal operations much less traumatic. Large organizations tend to be multivendor environments with PCs, laptops, mini and mainframe computers, and peripheral equipment. Standard and compatible equipment will provide users with backup data storage and processing capabilities if one machine should fail. Large-volume buyers may also find it easier to guarantee fast delivery from vendors in case of an emergency. Multivendor service providers often offer service and repair covering equipment made by many different companies.

In a one-computer organization, however, equipment failure and a long repair time could be disastrous. But standard/compatible equipment can be beneficial here too. If the local computer store had to special order an off-brand PC, a repair can be expected to take much longer than it would have if the equipment were standard models.

Whatever contingency plans for equipment exist, comparable plans for backup data files and processing procedures should also be in place. These should include identifying the critical wait time for repair before manual procedures are implemented to replace those that were done using the computer.

Part of good contingency planning is adequate backups of both data and programs. Along with the backup, however, procedures should be in place for restoring data and programs so processing can continue. Before processing continues, another copy of the backup should be made first so that the only copy of the data is not accidentally destroyed. Backup-scheduling software programs can be used to ensure a routine is followed. Also, mirroring software and data to a server or servers at one or more locations is another way to ensure valuable data isn't lost. There are also utility programs available that can recover seemingly lost data from disks. These utility programs should be purchased ahead of time and tested to make sure they can be used in an emergency.

Backup disks should be stored off-site, if possible. A small business may want to back up each day and put the day's backup in an office fireproof/media safe. Then, transfer the backup to a bank safe deposit box or vault the next day.

Adequate insurance coverage for both hardware and software should not be forgotten. Also, all serial numbers and software license information should be recorded and kept in a secure location.

POTENTIAL LEGAL LIABILITIES
FOR NOT HAVING A RECOVERY PLAN

Management should also be aware of the various sources of possible legal liability. First, there is the basic fiduciary duty to protect the assets of the enterprise. Second, there are federal statutes, including the Foreign Corrupt Practices Act (FCPA) and its requirements for recordkeeping and internal controls.

Legal sanctions could arise from a situation where there was a loss of records and data-processing operations. For example, a company is hit by a natural disaster that causes its data-processing operation to shut down and also destroys information processed and stored in the computer. The shutdown is severe and long enough to result in a loss of business to such an extent that survivability of the company is threatened.

In the above example, the data-processing performance breakdown could be seen as evidence of failure to "make and keep books, records, and accounts;" or as weak or nonexistent internal controls. The corporation's stockholders, faced with a substantial drop in their stock price, would probably see that the situation resulted from negligence on the part of corporate officers and sue.

While the FCPA does not mandate specific internal controls, company controls will be judged by whether or not they are reasonable under the circumstances for the operation of business. In other words, was it reasonable under the circumstances for our hypothetical company not to have a contingency plan? Theoretically, liability could befall the company if factual circumstances lead to the conclusion that, since the company was computer-dependent (assuming much of its accounts processing and record-keeping was computerized), it should have had contingency/disaster recovery planning to assure quick recovery of data-processing operations after a disaster.

With the FCPA, the burden of compliance lies in understanding the term *reasonable* and the actions, or lack thereof, that follow from this. In business practice, then, what is judged reasonable? Generally, a demonstration of reasonableness under the business judgment rule would be the presence of regular, competent, and periodic cost-benefit analyses of alternative contingency plans. Management should also be prepared to demonstrate that the disaster recovery plan was implemented, tested, reviewed, and if necessary, modified. An audit review attesting to this would strengthen management's claims.

The Comptroller of the Currency's requirement that all national banks have a disaster recovery plan is one of several legal obligations to insure that banks continue to operate. Other applicable laws for small businesses are contained in the Uniform Commercial Code and the Federal Electronic Funds Transfer Act.

The Employee Retirement Income Security Act of 1974 (ERISA) places statutory liabilities on anyone who is a benefit or pension plan fiduciary, such as business owners, directors, and officers. Severe business loss or insolvency resulting from a disaster may not affect these plans provided, of course, there is sufficient insurance coverage.

PROTECTING AND RETRIEVING CRITICAL RECORDS

Records, and their storage and retrieval, are massive problems for most companies. The first problem is to decide which records to store off-site. Next, how should they be cataloged, when should they be retrieved, and finally, when should they be destroyed.

Another consideration is that the media storage system should be compatible with the company's current system. A critical factor is the reliability of the media storage system.

Every company must have a system for the organization, control, storage, and retrieval of business records for their life cycle, particularly for the length of time required by law. This program should be integrated with the disaster recovery program.

Before deciding which records to be archived, either on tape, disk, hard drive, digital or optical image, paper, or microform, one should look first to company legal requirements. By state, federal, and local laws and regulations, companies are required to retain certain business records. Included are accounting and financial, administrative, corporate, legal, manufacturing, personnel, product, property, security, and tax records.

Business owners must be aware of the legal requirements that go with the creation and storage of electronic documents and records. These legal issues have become acute because of the growing demand by government agencies for records that prove or disprove a business's regulatory compliance.

Most business documents and records are either vital for business necessity, recovery, corporate memory, or compliance with state or federal laws and regulations.

Many company records are considered vital, such as trade secret and customer lists. Our present concern is with those records that, if destroyed, would seriously impair the company's ability to resume operations quickly. Such records would include accounts receivable, payroll files, billing records, customer master files, inventory, mailing lists, engineering and architectural drawings, and tax records. If these records are on the computer, the necessary duplicate program and operations documentation for processing should also be stored off-site.

Vital records have three essential elements: the information content; the processing activity; and the output function, the activity that results from processing—a billing mailed, for example. Vital records are also those records, that if destroyed, would seriously impair the company's ability to resume operations quickly.

It is important that the proper versions of the master files and the appropriate transaction records are cycled off-site to permit recovery.

In a data-processing disaster, it is normally the loss of information, or the inability to use that information when needed, that is most critical. Hardware losses are important, of course, but equipment can often be replaced easier and faster than information can be recovered.

Laws and regulations applicable to data storage and recovery seek to define the scope of information that a business must protect in order to produce certain records upon legitimate demand. A business must have those records to continue operating as a going concern. If the business cannot produce its records or continue to operate because records have been destroyed, then it is likely that questions of negligence and liability will be raised.

The federal government has over a thousand statutes and regulations that require organizations to have records management and protection and a workable disaster recovery plan. All laws and regulations covering an organization's activities should be researched to determine the kinds of records to retain and maintain.

CRITICAL STEPS IN DEVELOPING
A DISASTER RECOVERY PLAN

There are two questions that must be addressed in disaster recovery planning:

1. Where are we now?
   - What are our current company strengths, weaknesses, and limitations?
   - What major internal vulnerabilities do we face with our human, capital, information, and technological resources?
   - What external threats and hazards do we face?
   - What new opportunities for improvement exist in our protection measures, internal controls and security, and response capabilities?

2. Where will we be in one, two, and five years if we do nothing differently? Do we like these answers? If not, what are our options?

   - Do nothing.

   - Magnify, minify, modify, eliminate, enlarge, combine, re-arrange, put to other uses, etc.

   - Set long-range goals.

   - Set plan completion date.

   - Delegate somebody to be accountable for its implementation and testing.

   - Set date to review and refine the plan again.

The disaster recovery planning process begins with a delineation of the specific assets to be protected, classified, or categorized by asset type (capital, human, and information). The next step is to identify risks, list possible threats (i.e., natural, human, accident, and equipment-related) and the impact of each.

Remember, the top risks of damage or destruction to computers and network systems are: electronic or mechanical breakdowns, power variations or failure, computer hardware problems, communications/network failures, fire and related catastrophes, flood and water damage, and criminal acts such as vandalism, theft, and computer viruses. The following steps may counteract these risks:

- Estimate the probability of each of the above for your information systems and facility.

- Analyze your vulnerability to specific threats and the affect on information systems and business operations.

- Prepare a list and inventory of vital resources necessary for ongoing operations. Identify critical information.

- Examine business and legal priorities from purchasing, contract obligations, and records management that may be necessary for compliance or emergencies in recovery.

- Do a thorough review of insurance coverage—property loss, business interruption, and extra expenses.

- Prepare a written recovery plan that concentrates on the top hazards in frequency and dollar loss; these are fire, power failure, and water damage. Be prepared for total disaster. Assume the worst. The plan can always be scaled back for lesser emergencies. Balance cost vs. risk. No organization needs 100 percent redundancy for every function.

- Make sure everyone knows what to do. From senior management responsible for setting recovery in motion to team leaders in the field, everyone must know in advance what to do during a crisis.
- Determine the feasibility of the recovery plan. Test it periodically; evaluate and update it.
- If you have a back-up site, test the plan for coordination with the vendor and your suppliers.

Exhibit 13.1 is designed to help you calculate the approximate loss from time delays brought about by the occurrence of hazards, threats, and vulnerabilities. The impact data is then analyzed and a series of responses and emergency procedures are developed based on the criticality of each time loss scenario.

EXHIBIT 13.1
Disaster Planning Worksheet

Risk Event	Criticality of Assets Destroyed or Damaged	Probability of Occurrence	Probable Time Delay	Potential Direct Dollar Loss	Consequential Loss	Insurance Recovery	Net Loss	Current Costs of Protection

14

CYBERFRAUD AUDITS AND INVESTIGATIONS

To the lay person, fraud is simply lying, cheating, and possibly stealing, if guile or trickery are involved. Criminal fraud is a willful misrepresentation of a material fact with intent to deceive.

Lawyers tend to see fraud in three forms, *criminal*, *civil*, and *contractual*. Lawyers think of criminal fraud as a willful misrepresentation of a material fact with intent to deceive. The deception may involve some form of concealment. Civil fraud, to lawyers, is a misrepresentation of a material fact that causes damage (monetary or property loss). Lawyers view contractual fraud as involving a deception in the inducement of a contract or the execution of a contract. In any event, civil lawsuits can be brought for rescission of contract, recovery of property, or for damages, depending on the nature of the fraud.

RED FLAGS OF FRAUD

Red flags are signals, not proof, of fraud in and of themselves; they are accounting peculiarities or anomalies. Accountants and auditors see fraud from the perspectives of prevention, detection, and reporting of errors, irregularities, and oddities in books of account. The distinctions between errors, irregularities, and oddities are as follows:

- Errors are innocent mistakes, misinterpretations, or unintentional misstatements, usually immaterial in amount.
- Irregularities are intentional misstatements and omissions that are material in nature or amount.
- Oddities are transactions and account balances that occur too frequently or too rarely; or are too high or too low; or involve odd people, at odd places, and at odd times.

On the surface, red flags seem trivial in nature or amount. But there is something about them that doesn't square with history, reality, past practice, or good practice. For example, sharp rises and falls in certain key accounts like receivables, payables, inventory, and cash could give rise to an expanded audit scope. Or take as another example, changes in ratios of sales to cost of sales, receivables, inventory, freight in, freight out, and sales commissions paid. When these ratios deviate from long-term trends, you may wish to further analyze the accounts.

Other red flags or events or conditions in the firm that give rise to suspicions that a motive may exist to falsify records (i.e., to raise, lower, or omit data) may include weakening sales, recurring cash shortages, an unfair reward system, high turnover of employees and managers, high turnover of audit and law firms.

When errors, irregularities and oddities are evident in the course of an audit, there may be a responsibility for auditors (internal or external) to report their concerns to senior management, the Audit Committee of the Board of Directors, or the Board itself.

PREVENTING CYBERFRAUD

The prevention of fraud in books of account requires tight internal controls, able and ethical management, honest employees, and perhaps a measure of good luck, since no accounting or management system can be made totally fraud-proof.

Criminologists and organizational psychologists suggest that fraud, theft, and embezzlement by organizational employees can be understood by studying the individuals who commit such crimes and the environments in which they work. Criminologists say a typical embezzler, for example, is a person who holds a position of trust, has an unshareable financial burden, and rationalizes his or her defalcations as borrowing, not stealing. Organizational psychologists would add that such behavior is more prevalent in organizations with low trust and autocratic managers who are poor role models for honesty. A work environment that is physically unsafe and economically unstable also adds to the risk of employee theft, fraud, and embezzlement, as do such things like loose controls (easy access to assets and records) and lax management.

The separation of principle duties and the audit trail requirement were the main defenses against employee fraud in manual systems, and they persist in new form today. Separation now means segregating the work efforts of computer operators from systems analysts, from programmers (who write instructions so that the systems will operate efficiently and correctly as designed), and from people who enter data into the system. The audit trail now consists not of supporting documents (stock requisitions, purchase orders, receiving reports, invoices), but of history files, programs, flowcharts, and procedures.

FINANCIAL vs. FRAUD AUDITING

Financial auditing is a methodology intended to evaluate the level of accuracy, timeliness, and completeness of the recordings of business transactions. However, auditors do not review all transactions. Tests of accuracy, timeliness, and completeness are accomplished by sampling techniques. The purpose of such testing is to determine whether transaction data is free of material error and that financial statements are accordingly free of material misstatement.

Fraud auditing (also called forensic accounting), while borrowing many techniques from financial auditing, is more of a mindset than a methodology. It relies on creativity as much as it does on reasoning. Indeed, it requires that the fraud auditor thinks (not acts) like a thief by considering questions like: Where are the weakest links in the chain of controls? How can I attack them without drawing attention? How can I destroy the evidence of my attack? What powers do I have that I can enlarge on? What plausible explanation can I give if someone gets suspicious of my activities? If I am apprehended, how can I explain away my conduct? The more a fraud auditor can learn to think like a thief, the better his or her effort to detect fraud.

Financial and fraud auditing differ also in the degree of concern for evidence of material error or misstatement. While the materiality rule in financial auditing has its place in a cost/benefit context, materiality is not a guiding principle in fraud auditing. The amount of a visible fraud may be small, but most frauds in books of account are like icebergs—the biggest part is below the surface. Discovering even small discrepancies can give rise to uncovering large defalcations. That's one reason why auditors often say they discover fraud by accident, not by audit plan or design.

In truth, the discovery of fraud is generally no accident. It comes from diligent effort and an auditor's basic assumption that if fraud is there, he or she is determined to find it. Are all frauds in books of account found or discovered on the basis of detected discrepancies? No. Many frauds surface on the basis of allegations or complaints by co-workers, co-conspirators on the inside and outside, customers, competitors, suppliers, or prospective suppliers.

What form do frauds in books of account generally take? In simplest form, frauds involve cash receipts or disbursements and are accomplished by creating fake debits or credits. Fake debits are generally disguised as purchases or accounts payable so that an offsetting credit can be posted to cash. Fake credits are generally disguised as returns and allowances and posted to accounts receivable. The proceeds are then split between an insider and the customer who derives the financial benefit.

Perhaps the most difficult frauds to uncover and prosecute are those that involve small amounts on a frequent or cyclical basis. Perhaps the more difficult frauds to uncover and prosecute are those that involve small amounts on a frequent or cyclical basis. Cash lapping ("borrowing" from today's cash sales on the hope of replacing it tomorrow) is one such technique. Skimming (intercepting cash before it gets counted or entered) is a related practice. These two practices give the thieves a measure of defense in a prosecution for larceny or embezzlement because it seems to a jury that the culprit had no intention of "permanently depriving" the owner of his or her property. Intent to permanently deprive is an element of proof required in criminal prosecutions for larceny in some states.

Many of the frauds in books of account are committed in small businesses by a single person in an accounting role, who is unsupervised, and who has easy access to company assets and records. In larger organizations, where internal controls are better but still not adequate, two or more employees may have to conspire to commit fraud.

In very large companies, frauds in books of account are often committed by upper level managers (i.e., profit-center directors and their staffs). Their intent is not necessarily to steal but to manipulate data to enhance profitability and thereby earn higher bonuses, or impress the brass at headquarters, or to comply with goals imposed on the profit center by senior management.

At the top management level of public companies, much of the accounting skullduggery is intended to impress stockholders or lenders. Accordingly, profits are arbitrarily raised and costs are arbitrarily lowered by such techniques as plugging sales or ending inventory, capitalizing current expenses, deferring necessary repairs, etc.

Fraud auditing concentrates on account analyses, trend watching, pattern recognition, and monitoring and testing for processing exceptions. Fraud auditing concentrates less on sampling transactions and checklist completions. It requires that one be able to see through the chaos of accounting systems for non-random events.

The chaos theory holds that there is order even in chaos. Fraud auditing teaches us to be alert and look above, below, and beyond the chaos to understand what is really happening in an accounting system. Random error may not be random at all; it may follow a jagged course. It does have a pattern, but not the typical symmetrical patterns we are so accustomed to in the world of debits, credits, and trial balances.

CYBERFRAUDS IN ACCOUNTING INFORMATION SYSTEMS

Audit techniques involving computers are called audit around and audit through. The audit around technique provides checks to determine whether data entering the computer (input) matches data leaving the computer (output). Here dollar totals and hash totals are compared at both entry and output stages. If they agree, the auditor assumes no incorrection has occurred. But data can be manipulated while it's running through the computer as well as being manipulated at the time of entry, so the more acceptable technique for auditing computerized accounting systems is the audit through technique. Here, the auditor must understand programming logic. For example, in the audit around approach, the auditor would merely know that what went in the computer in terms of totals came out with equal totals. If a payroll program is written so that small sums are withdrawn from each employee's check and accumulated and added to the programmer's own salary check, the auditor wouldn't know that. The total payroll amount was not changed, nor was the total number of payroll checks issued. This form of fraud is referred to as *salami slicing*. Taking a little off each check won't arouse anyone's curiosity and it is generally undetectable, if the audit-around approach is used, ergo, the need to conduct audits through the computer. It is just as important to see what is happening inside the black box as it is to see what happens outside the box.

The logic built into accounting application programs is based on a chain of events which take place in a normal business transaction. The system of logic used in such programs is in essence based on general rules and standard operating procedures (SOPs) or policies.

In a well-organized, well-managed, and stable organizational environment, these general rules or SOPs account for the large majority of transactions. Exceptions or deviations are the rarities. In environments where crisis and chaos abound — unstable conditions, poor management, poor organization or work — transactions are handled on an ad hoc basis. Everything is an exception. There are no general rules, or if they exist, they are venerated more in their breach than in their compliance.

In such unstable environments, opportunities for theft, fraud, and embezzlement abound. Internal controls, if they exist at all, are there for pretense purposes: to give the appearance or illusion of control.

Even in reasonably well-managed firms, exceptions are bound to occur. Human error alone will account for a large measure of these exceptions. Corrections are then made and things then go on as planned or as usual.

In environments in which computers are utilized for accounting and particularly in on-line and distributed systems, the chance or probability for error is magnified by the complexity of the systems. Accommodations for regular errors such as suspense accounts, unresolved differences, unclassified expenditures, unknown vendors, unknown payees, payables suspense accounts, receivables suspense, inventory variation accounts, etc. are provided for in the system's programming. In such environments, data can be processed much faster than human minds can take corrective actions for past processing errors. There are always large amounts of money, represented by assets either bought, sold, or disposed of which can't be fully accounted for at any given time.

Now enter the thief. In such chaos (chaos is a relative term here, meaning many items moving through which can't yet be correctly classified as to account title, i.e., expense or revenue category, asset or liability category), even a semi-literate thief can have a field day. Patching and plugging holes keeps the data processing department so busy that an ultimate system of controls is never developed.

A patchwork quilt or pastiche of controls is the best that can be designed.

With such looseness in internal controls, our thief doesn't need to have much imagination to exploit weaknesses. If inventory postings are already running two weeks behind, no one will be the wiser if a stevedore on the loading dock validates a shipment as fully received, when in fact it is short one or two boxes, one or two skids, or one or two barrels. Such sloppiness in work habits can then lead to an even more serious problem: why not take a box home or share the loot with a confederate, like a truck driver, receiving dock supervisor, or work colleague?

In analyzing accounts and reviewing transactions, the auditor must be keenly aware that the danger of fraud lies not with "normal" transactions but with the exceptions, the deviations from normal, if there is such a thing in the environment under audit.

Investigators too must become acutely aware of what is normal and abnormal in accounting systems and internal controls. These deviations from the usual course of business events represent the greatest potential threat for employee fraud because they permit easy over-rides and by-passes of controls. If you can't fabricate a whole transaction, you can always fabricate an emergency or create a distraction to justify deviation at some intermediate step in the processing of the transaction.

Conclusions

Fraud in a computerized accounting system can occur at any of the three stages of processing, input, throughput, or output. Input scams are the simplest to accomplish and therefore the most prevalent of the three. Input scams involve the addition, alteration, forgery, or counterfeiting of data at the input stage of processing. An input scam can consist of the omission of data too.

Throughput scams involve the exploitation of weaknesses in operating system controls at the throughput phase. For example, a trapdoor or Trojan horse may be left in the operating system so that the errant user can access the system at will, assume the identity of others, or take on superuser privileges, thereby burying his tracks. The errant programmer can steal files or programs and hold them for ransom—or even plant worms, viruses, and time bombs. Needless to say, throughput scams, in order of criticality, are the most worrisome of the three.

Output scams consist of suppressing or destroying records like exceptions logs to cover up fraud. Output scams may also involve theft of confidential data to sell to competitors, like customer lists and R&D results.

INVESTIGATING CYBERFRAUD

In computer crimes (fraud, larceny, embezzlement, sabotage of equipment, or information theft), we often don't know what specific crime was committed, by whom it was committed, or worse yet, how it was committed.

The "how" factor of criminal investigations is often a matter left to forensics experts. Clues are analyzed to determine how the crime was committed in the hope that the analysis may provide some insight on the identity of the likely culprit.

Auditing and accounting are the most useful tools in the investigation of computer-related crimes, at least of those which involve thefts of tangible assets and where computer systems have been used as means and instruments for the execution of the crime.

Therefore, investigators of computer crimes must have at least a general knowledge of accounting and auditing principles and techniques, as well as some understanding of how computers and controls operate with respect to the recording of financial transactions and financial information.

However, if fraudulent messages are transmitted in proper form and amount, the above controls will not detect them. The same was true in manual accounting systems. Fraudulent or forged documents were no more discernible than they are now in computerized systems. Good controls discourage fraud but can't prevent it.

INTERNAL INVESTIGATIONS POLICY AND PROCEDURE

Once an offense has been discovered, though not fully verified, the company should start an internal investigation to determine if the incident should be reported to law enforcement, other government authorities, or your insurance company.

Responding quickly to a suspected offense, gathering evidence and punishing personnel swiftly and drastically could be a fatal error. Everyone involved in an internal investigation must be aware of the company's policy and strategy on internal investigations, the laws that could have been violated by company personnel, and laws affecting the gathering of information and evidence.

Every organization should have an internal investigation game plan. This means, first, a board of directors resolution or a policy directive from management that clarifies and answers these questions:

- What misconduct (broadly defined and at what level) will trigger an internal investigation?
- To whom should the incident or misconduct be reported?
- When should an investigation be initiated?
- Who should conduct the internal investigation and under what circumstances?
- What should be the purpose of the investigation?
- What types of disclosures are mandatory?

Corporate management must take the lead for several reasons. First, there may be legal disclosure and reporting requirements. Second, a reporting and investigation policy sets up a formal system for handling incidents as well as giving management another form of control over corporate-wide activities.

Directing the Investigation

The following outline suggests critical initial steps in an internal corporate investigation. This outline starts from the premise that an internal investigation is necessary, that a decision has been made to learn the extent and seriousness of a specific corporate problem—a problem that may or may not, at some point, lead to the notification and involvement of government or criminal justice agencies.

The objectives of this outline are to provide guidance on conducting a prompt, efficient, and diligent investigation, and that offers maximum legal protection to the corporate entity. The Board of Directors or the owner(s) of the corporation may want to appoint a special committee to direct the investigation and retain outside counsel.

An enabling resolution by the Board should be drafted and say that the special committee will direct a legal study and investigation and that it should retain outside legal counsel to provide the corporation, through the special committee, legal advice based on its findings.

Outside legal counsel should be authorized to conduct the investigation and be:

- Given autonomy to conduct a professional investigation and inquiry
- Authorized to procure assistance as necessary, such as independent accountants and investigators
- Authorized to interview any employees of the corporation who might know the facts
- Authorized to analyze any and all information gathered from sources and materials inside and outside the corporation

Outside counsel should meet on a regular basis with the special committee. Minutes or some record of the meetings should be made. Obvious sensitive topics need not be recorded. Some evidence of these meetings is needed, however, to establish the diligence of the special committee and counsel.

Reporting responsibility on the investigation should be only to the special committee. Legal counsel at all times must make decisions on assistance and investigative materials based on the attorney-client privilege and work product rule. If company personnel are used in the investigation, they must be instructed that during the investigation their work product and findings are to be given only to the outside legal counsel.

Independent accountants, auditors, investigators, and others should be engaged to assist and report exclusively to the outside legal counsel. Again, such engagements should be set up so as not to jeopardize the attorney-client privilege or work product rule. Services of independent experts should be procured through outside counsel and the work done under its direction.

Results of the work should become the exclusive property of the outside law firm; all communications are exclusively with outside counsel, and all professional services paid for by the outside counsel.

All of the above should be included in a retainer letter or contract between the law firm and the independent service supplier.

At the conclusion of the investigation, outside counsel advises the special committee, the company owner(s), or the Board of Directors on its findings, suggests legal action, and decides what action, if any, to take.

15

INSURANCE FOR CYBERFRAUD AND CYBERTORTS

The securing of appropriate and comprehensive insurance protection and coverage for the risks of loss of business or liability exposure is a very important line of defense. Insurance complements policies and internal controls; however, insurance should never be seen as a substitute for other protective measures. Employee dishonesty insurance and fidelity bonds are not a substitute for internal and accounting controls, but internal controls and audits do not necessarily prevent and detect employee dishonesty and losses.

REASONS FOR INSURANCE

The purpose of insurance is to indemnify the business owner/ employer for loss of money, property, or other assets sustained through acts of nature, personnel, or outsiders. The scope of acts insured against may include: property loss or damage, business interruption/economic loss, disaster-related costs, copyright or trademark infringement, libel or slander, sexual harassment, invasion of privacy, unfair competition, embezzlement, forgery or alteration, extortion, counterfeit currency, computer systems fraud, or other fraudulent and dishonest acts.

TYPES OF COMPUTER INSURANCE POLICIES

There are a number of policies to cover the above acts. For computer equipment, it is best to get separate coverage rather than rely on a general business policy. Be sure to get replacement cost coverage that pays to repair or replace damaged equipment at current prices. The policy should provide for the reproduction or replacement of lost data or media or electronic damage recovery.

Business interruption insurance will cover loss of sales or revenue due to a disaster, and, perhaps, computer crash losses, or losses related to jammed Internet sites. Look at extra expense insurance for reimbursement of disaster-related costs over and above your normal operating expenses; policies may also cover salaries, taxes, rent, and claims preparation costs.

There are policies that provide commercial banks and other depository institutions with coverage for crimes involving computers or other electronic equipment committed by people outside their organizations. The policy can be purchased in addition to a financial institution bond, which covers computer theft or fraud by employees. The policy expands upon that coverage to include third-party fraud and other technological exposures, such as losses from computer viruses, software piracy, toll-call fraud, and high-tech extortion. The policy also covers fraud involving computer systems, computer programs, voice-initiated money transfers, forged faxes, and electronic communications to the institution. In addition, it covers legal liability for service bureau operations and electronic communications from the institution; breaches of security for credit cards; and damage or destruction of programs and data. You might want the policy to cover costs related to the legal liability of loss of computer capability or operational errors that produce inaccurate data or delayed processing for customers.

Specific website-related policies are becoming available to cover or augment general liability policies for online defamation, slander, and libel.

Patent infringement liability insurance is designed to protect a company that "unintentionally manufactures, uses, distributes, or advertises a patented article."

Patent, copyright, trade dress, and trademark infringement cases plus domain name disputes have exploded in the last decade. Infringement cases can be expensive, usually exceeding $250,000 for each party. Before buying the infringement coverage, however, check your regular comprehensive general liability insurance policy's declarations sheet, specifically "Coverage B" which may have "advertising" injury coverage. Legal defense costs may be reimbursed by your insurance company under this clause.

A recent policy covers financial losses from the theft of trade secrets. The secrets must be owned by the company and be in a recorded form.

EMPLOYMENT PRACTICES LIABILITY INSURANCE

The distribution of standard anti-discrimination statements in employee handbooks is not enough to fend off claims. Education and sensitivity training are important, but by themselves cannot eliminate discrimination in the workplace. By using prevention techniques like training and education as well as the strategic use of employment practices liability (EPL) insurance, employers can implement a more effective program to reduce liabilities.

EMPLOYEE DISHONESTY INSURANCE

The purpose of employee dishonesty insurance is to indemnify the employer for loss of money or other property sustained through dishonest acts of the employer's bonded personnel. The scope of acts insured against may include: larceny, theft of money and securities, embezzlement, forgery or alteration, misappropriation, wrongful abstraction, willful misapplication, extortion, counterfeit currency, computer systems fraud, or other fraudulent and dishonest acts committed by the employee, whether acting alone or in collusion with others.

Bear in mind that the fidelity bond is not an all-risk form. Loss must result from dishonesty on the part of the bonded employee. Loss caused by omission or error not involving dishonesty is not covered.

Property, real or personal—including money—is covered, whether owned by the employer or belonging to others. If an employee had access to funds or if he is authorized to buy, sell, ship, or store goods, that employee should be bonded in an amount adequate to offset potential thefts. It is logical enough that the larger the firm's assets and the greater the turnover in volume of business, the more probable that a larger loss or series of losses may be concealed for a long period.

The insurance is written on a schedule basis, that is, to cover employees by name or position, or on a blanket coverage of all employees.

Under the Employee Retirement Income Security Act of 1974 (ERISA) every company subject to its provisions is required to have employee dishonesty insurance for anyone handling an employer-sponsored welfare or pension benefit plan, including the plan sponsor, administrator, trustee, officer, or employee who handles funds or other property of the plan.

READING THE FINE PRINT

With any insurance policy evaluate and examine: specifically excepted or excluded perils, proposed endorsements, limits of liability, required proof, duty to defend, notice, and establishing damage/loss figures.

Required Proof

For example, to satisfy an embezzlement claim, circumstantial evidence must show that the employee intended to defraud or embezzle (a voluntary act resulting in direct financial gain).

The "manifest intent" clause of policies can be shown when a particular result is certain to follow from an employee's conduct. However, there must be more than mistake, carelessness, or incompetence.

A proof of loss document, signed and sworn to by the insured, is usually required by the insurance policy.

Notice

The notice provision is included in nearly every insurance policy, and is a potential pitfall in obtaining coverage for claims. Under an insurance policy, notice is required to the insurance company, within a reasonable time, of a claim for recovery. Failure to satisfy this requirement can result in no indemnification for an otherwise covered claim.

The notice provision is usually in the conditions section of a policy. Terms used to define notice are often: as soon as practicable after an incident that could be eligible for a claim; or, as soon thereafter as the insured has knowledge of an incident; or, immediately.

Notice is often refused or delayed because the insured is not sure of the proper insurance policy under which to make a claim, is ignorant of the policy coverage, lacks knowledge of the incident, or does not believe a claim will arise.

However, once it is determined that notice should be given for a claim, it is best to inform the insurance company in writing as quickly as possible. In fact, even if the organization is unsure that its insurance will cover a claim, it is best to notify the insurance company of the possible claim, and include information about the time, place, and circumstances of the loss.

Duty to Defend

Make sure the insurance company will defend an entire action if any part of the claim is within its insurance coverage.

Damages and the Rule of Certainty

Under this rule, the plaintiff must establish exact damages without recourse to speculation and conjecture—and show a direct chain of causation running from the event to the loss sustained.

The problem with computer-related damage claims is establishing the value of information.

NINE STEPS IN RECOVERY FOR LOSSES

1. Consult with your attorney or insurance broker regarding:
   - Identify the specific policy under which you can file a claim.
   - Clarify meanings of specific clauses relating to notice, subrogation (settlement) remedies, proof of loss, and the time frame for submitting the proof according to your specific policy.
   - Identify what types of damages are excluded in your policy.

2. Send notice of loss immediately to your broker/agent.

3. Investigate the possible loss:
   - Use internal auditors, accountants, security and legal personnel, or go to an outside claims investigative agency specializing in computer-related damages or information loss. Cooperate with insurance company investigators at the appropriate point.
   - Identify and interview all staff with knowledge of the incident.
   - Identify documents, electronic media, and other materials that might be relevant to determining loss or guilty parties.
   - Determine the extent of the loss and if any assets are retrievable.

4. Terminate the employee(s) involved in an illegal act—only on the advice of legal counsel and if your policy has a termination clause that excludes coverage if you retain a dishonest employee.

5. Submit proof of loss to the insurance company.

6. Again, cooperate with your insurance company; do not let them charge that your company failed to cooperate with the investigation in any way. However, consult with your attorney about the nature of your cooperation, especially about the confidentiality of documents.

7. Do not settle with any party without discussing it with your insurance company.

8. Present accurate and provable/auditable losses in your claim.

9. Be prepared to sue your insurance company if your claim is denied.

APPENDIX A

FEDERAL STATUTES ON COMPUTER-RELATED CRIME

COMPUTER FRAUD AND ABUSE ACT OF 1986

This Act has become the key federal statute for information security and prosecution of computer-related crime. Expanded liability for computer-related fraud and provisions for civil remedies are provided in the 1994 amendments to the Act. The amendments also provide a lower standard of liability for those who knowingly access a computer without authorization and those who commit acts with a reckless disregard of a substantial and unjustifiable risk to a computer or computer system.

The National Information Infrastructure Protection Act of 1996 became Public Law 104-294 in October 1996. The Act amends the Computer Fraud and Abuse Act, Title 18 U.S.C., Section 1030. The amendments increase protection of the national information infrastructure; criminalize access by government employees who exceed their authority to access government information; and extend protection to computers and communication used in interstate or foreign commerce.

New subsections ((e)(8) through (e)(8)(D)) to the code include a definition of *damage* meaning "any impairment to the integrity or availability of data, a program, a system, or information that: causes loss aggregating at least $5,000 in value during any one-year period to one or more individuals; modifies, impairs, or potentially modifies or impairs, the medical examination, diagnosis, treatment, or care of one or more individuals; causes physical injury to any person; or threatens public health or safety."[1]

Amendments to the Act criminalize access by government employees who exceed or abuse their authority to access and obtain

---

[1] Public Law 104-294. The National Information Infrastructure Protection Act.

government and private sector information; criminalize extortion by a person or firm who transmits "any communication in interstate or foreign commerce containing any threat to cause damage to a protected computer."[2] *Obtaining information* includes simply reading the information, as well as copying or stealing it.

The amendments change the punishment for offenses committed for purposes of commercial advantage or private financial gain or in furtherance of any criminal or tortuous act in violation of federal or state law. These offenses carry a fine or imprisonment of not more than five years or both.

In the computer definition section, *federal interest* is interpreted for protected computer meaning to include government or financial institution computers and any computer used in interstate or foreign commerce or communication.

ELECTRONIC COMMUNICATIONS PRIVACY ACT
(Public Law 99-508, 18 U.S.C. Sec. 2510–2520 and 2701–2710)

The federal electronic surveillance statutes were originally enacted as Title III of the Omnibus Crime Control and Safe Streets Act of 1968 and amended by the Electronic Communications Privacy Act of 1986 (ECPA). ECPA extends the protection of the Wiretap Act of 1968 to electronic communications and communications systems, including radio, satellite, and data communications. Excluded from coverage is any radio transmission readily accessible to the general public and types of protected radio signals.

ECPA protects the privacy of transmitted and stored electronic communications from interception and disclosure. The Act covers electronic communications made by "any transfer of signs, signals, writings, images, sounds, data, or intelligence of any nature transmitted in whole or in part by a wire, radio, electromagnetic, photoelectronic or photo-optical system that affects interstate or foreign commerce."[3] The only requirement of the Act is that the information affect interstate or foreign commerce. The Act applies to government, private, and public systems, exempting those systems without any expectation of privacy.

---

[2] Public Law 104-294. The National Information Infrastructure Protection Act.

[3] Public Law 99-508, 18 U.S.C. Sec. 2510–2520 and 2701–2710. Electronic Communications Privacy Act.

Under ECPA, it is illegal to intercept electronic communications or to use or disclose the contents to another person. Further, it is a felony carrying fines and prison terms. The party whose communication was intercepted can bring suit in federal court; penalties are greater when the interception was for commercial advantage or illegal purpose and the plaintiff may recover actual damages and profits made as a result of the violation.

The privacy of electronic mail is protected under the law, with a misdemeanor penalty for those who break into an electronic communications system holding messages. ECPA covers any service "which provides to users thereof the ability to send or receive wire or electronic communications." A remote computing service is a system that provides public computer communications storage or processing. Also covered is "any person or entity providing the wire or electronic communication service." A key and implied element is that the system be configured for privacy.

Offenses committed for commercial advantage or malicious destruction or damage carry a fine of up to $250,000, a one-year prison term, or both.

For both stored and transmitted communications, the intent standard as described in the above computer crime law applies to any defendant; that is, it must be proven that the defendant intentionally sought to intercept, alter, damage, or destroy the data communication or message.

For providers of electronic communications services to the public, it is illegal to divulge knowingly the contents of any communication except to the sender or intended recipient of the information.

As noted above, ECPA broadened the definition of communications to include electronic communications, including computers, fax machines, and paging devices.

Stored Electronic Communications

ECPA protection extends to electronic communications stored after transmission. Requirements for government access are set forth in 18 USC 2703–2705: a search warrant issued under the Federal Rules of Criminal Procedure (Rule 41, search and seizure) or equivalent state warrant. The government can also use an administrative subpoena authorized by a federal or state statute, or a federal or state grand jury, or trial subpoena. Another avenue is via a court order for disclosure if the government can show "there is reason to believe the contents of a wire or electronic communication, or the records or other information sought, are relevant to a legitimate law enforcement inquiry."[4]

Counterfeit Access Devices

When Congress passed the counterfeit access device law (18 U.S.C. Section 1029) to prohibit the use of access devices to carry out fraud and other crimes, it was focusing primarily on credit card fraud. However, the law was intended to be broad enough to encompass technological advances, including, for example, telephone and cellular access codes.

In *United States v. Fernandez* the court held that computer passwords met the definition of an access device that, if possessed and used with the intent to defraud, could come under 18 U.S.C. Sec. 1029. The statute also reached fraudulent uses of telephone access codes or credit card account numbers.

DROP-DEAD FUNCTIONS

Tucked away in the Omnibus Crime Bill is an important amendment to the Computer Fraud and Abuse Act (CFAA), 18 U.S.C. Sec. 1030. Section 290001 of the Crime Bill contains the Computer Abuse Amendments Act of 1994. This act prohibits the knowing transmission of a program, information, code, or command to a computer or computer system that is intended to damage, deny, or interrupt a computer or a computer system. This act applies when the harmful transmission occurs without the authorization of the computer system owner and results in damage of $1,000 or more in any one-year period.

Also prohibited is the transmission of codes or commands if done "with reckless disregard of a substantial and unjustifiable risk" that the transmission damage or deny the use of a computer, computer system, network, computer program, or data. Penalties include a fine, one year in prison, or both.

---

[4] Federal Rule of Criminal Procedure no. 41.

PROVISIONS OF THE AMENDMENTS

A civil action section is added whereby any person who suffers damage from a person who knowingly causes a malicious transmission "may maintain a civil action against the violator to obtain compensatory damages and injunctive relief or other equitable relief."[5] A malicious transmission caused by "reckless disregard" can bring only economic damages.

Actions brought under this amendment must be within two years of the date of the act complained of or the date of the discovery of the damage.

The last change was to insert "adversely" in Section 1030(a)(3) to read: " . . . and such conduct [intentional and unauthorized access] adversely affects the use of the Government's operation of such computer."

DEFINITIONS OF TERMS IN THE AMENDMENTS

Turning to the terms used in the amendments, the term "a computer used in interstate commerce or communications" is broader than "federal interest" computer.

"Knowingly causes," means acting with knowledge, is cognizant, or aware of the nature of one's conduct.

"Reckless disregard" refers to a lack of due caution, heedless indifference, or a "substantial and unjustifiable risk." It would have to be defined based on the situation.

Use of the terms "program, information, code, or command" include more than logic bombs, and should cover worms, viruses, or any harmful device or function.

SENTENCING GUIDELINES FOR INDIVIDUALS CHARGED WITH COMPUTER-RELATED FRAUD

The United States Sentencing Commission has prepared the sentencing guidelines for federal crimes. The Commission was established by the Sentencing Reform Act of 1984 and charged with

---

[5] 18 U.S.C. Sec. 1030. Omnibus Crime Bill.

drafting guidelines for federal judges to use when sentencing convicted defendants. The objective of the Act was an effective, fair
sentencing system. Congress sought to obtain honesty, reasonable
uniformity, and proportionality in sentencing. Honesty means the
sentence imposed by the court is the sentence the offender will
serve; abolishing parole was one method to this end. Narrowing
the wide disparity in sentences imposed for similar criminal
offenses committed by similar offenders is a way to achieve reasonable uniformity. Imposing appropriately different sentences for
criminal conduct of differing severity could achieve the objective
of proportionality in sentencing.

The Act directs the Commission to create categories of offense
behavior and offender characteristics. In 1986, the Commission
asked for and got legislation to deal with issuance of general policy
statements concerning imposition of fines, the permissible width
of a guideline range calling for a term of imprisonment, and appellate review of sentences.

A federal court must select a sentence from within the guideline
range. In an atypical case, the court is allowed a departure from the
guideline, but must specify reasons for the departure; an appellate
court may review such a departure.

THE SENTENCING TABLE AND INSTRUCTIONS

The Commission has established a sentencing table that, for technical and practical reasons, contains 43 levels. Each level in the
table prescribes ranges that overlap with the ranges in the preced-
ing and succeeding levels.

In applying the guidelines, one must first determine the applicable offense guideline section. For example, for computer-related
fraud, 18 USC 1029 and 1030, this would be Part F, Offenses Involving Fraud or Deceit, 2F1.1.

Next, determine the base offense level and apply any appropriate specific offense characteristics contained in the particular
guideline. Each offense may cover one statute or many and has a
corresponding base offense level and may have one or more specific characteristics that adjust the offense level upward or down-
ward. Other instructions must be applied depending on the
particular offense and case.

THE SENTENCING TABLE AND INSTRUCTIONS

Exhibit A.1 presents the guidelines for fraud, including computer-related fraud, with comments on sentencing-related cases and instructions. The guidelines are designed to apply to a wide variety of fraud cases. The statutory maximum term of imprisonment for most such offenses is five years. The guidelines do not link offense characteristics to specific code sections. Because federal fraud statutes are so broadly written, a single pattern of offense conduct usually can be prosecuted under several code sections. As a result, the offense of conviction may be somewhat arbitrary. Furthermore, most fraud statutes cover a broad range of conduct with extreme variation in severity.

Empirical analyses of pre-guidelines practices showed that the most important factors that determined sentence length were the amount of loss and whether the offense was an isolated crime of opportunity or was sophisticated or repeated. Accordingly, although they are imperfect, these are the primary factors upon which the guidelines have been based.

Sentence Guideline Application Notes

The extent to which an offense is planned or sophisticated is important in assessing its potential harmfulness and the level of danger of the offender, independent of actual harm. A complex scheme or repeated incidents of fraud are indicative of an intention and potential to do considerable harm. In pre-guidelines practice, this factor had a significant impact, especially in frauds involving small losses. Accordingly, the guidelines specify a two-level enhancement when this factor is present.

A defendant who has been subject to civil or administrative proceedings for the same or similar fraudulent conduct demonstrates aggravated criminal intent and deserves additional punishment for not conforming with the requirements of judicial process or orders issued by federal, state, or local administrative agencies.

Offenses that involve the use of transactions or accounts outside the United States in an effort to conceal illicit profits and criminal conduct involve a particularly high level of sophistication and complexity. These offenses are difficult to detect and require costly investigations and prosecutions. Consequently, a minimum level of 12 is provided for these offenses.

EXHIBIT A.1
Offenses Involving Computer-Related Fraud

(a) Base Offense Level: 6
(b) Specific Offense Characteristics
    (1) If the loss exceeded $2,000, increase the offense level as follows:

Loss (Apply the Greatest)		Increase in Level
A.	$2,000 or less	no increase
B.	more than $2,000	add 1
C.	more than $5,000	add 2
D.	more than $10,000	add 3
E.	more than $20,000	add 4
F.	more than $40,000	add 5
G.	more than $70,000	add 6
H.	more than $120,000	add 7
I.	more than $200,000	add 8
J.	more than $350,000	add 9
K.	more than $500,000	add 10
L.	more than $800,000	add 11
M.	more than $1,500,000	add 12
N.	more than $2,500,000	add 13
O.	more than $5,000,000	add 14
P.	more than $10,000,000	add 15
Q.	more than $20,000,000	add 16
R.	more than $40,000,000	add 17
S.	more than $80,000,000	add 18

(2) If the offense involved (a) more than minimal planning or (b) a scheme to defraud more than one victim, increase by 2 levels.

(3) If the offense involved (a) a misrepresentation that the defendant was acting on behalf of a charitable, educational, religious or political organization, or a government agency, or (b) violation of any judicial or administrative order, injunction, decree, or process not addressed elsewhere in the guidelines, increase by 2 levels. If the resulting offense level is less than level 10, increase to level 10.

(4) If the offense involved the conscious or reckless risk of serious bodily injury, increase by 2 levels. If the resulting offense level is less than level 13, increase to level 13.

(5) If the offense involved the use of foreign bank accounts or transactions to conceal the true nature or extent of the fraudulent conduct, and the offense level as determined above is less than 12, increase to level 12.

(6) If the offense (a) substantially jeopardized the safety and soundness of a financial institution or (b) affected a financial institution and the defendant derived more than $1,000,000 in gross receipts from the offense, increase by 4 levels. If the resulting offense level is less than level 24, increase to level 24.

"More than minimal planning"[6] means the offense required more planning than is typical for commission of the offense in a simpler form. It also applies if significant affirmative steps were taken to conceal the offense. "More than minimal planning" is deemed present in any case involving repeated acts over a period of time, unless it is clear that each instance was purely opportune.

"Scheme to defraud more than one victim"[7] refers to a design or plan to obtain something of value from more than one person. In this context, *victim* refers to the person or entity from which the funds are to come directly.

The base offense level for 18 U.S.C. Sec. 1030(a)(1), "knowingly accesses a computer . . . and obtains information. . ." is set at 35 if the information is top secret; at 30 for all other national defense information. *Top secret information* is defined as information that, if disclosed, "reasonably could be expected to cause exceptionally grave damage to the national security." This is from Executive Order 12356.

In the case of an offense involving false identification documents or access devices, an upward departure may be warranted where the actual loss does not adequately reflect the seriousness of the conduct.

An offense shall be deemed to have "substantially jeopardized the safety and soundness of a financial institution"[8] if, as a consequence of the offense, the institution became insolvent; substantially reduced benefits to pensioners or insured; was unable on demand to refund fully any deposit, payment, or investment; was so depleted of its assets as to be forced to merge with another institution in order to continue active operations; or was placed in substantial jeopardy of any of the above.

"Gross receipts from the offense"[9] includes all property, real or personal, tangible or intangible, which is obtained directly or indirectly as a result of such offense.

---

[6] United States Sentencing Commission Guidelines subsection (b)(2)(a).

[7] United States Sentencing Commission Guidelines subsection (b)(2)(B).

[8] United States Sentencing Commission Guidelines subsection (b)(6)(a).

[9] United States Sentencing Commission Guidelines subsection (b)(6)(b).

CRITERIA FOR UPWARD OR DOWNWARD
ADJUSTMENTS AND DEPARTURES

Adjustments to the offense level are based upon the role the defendant played in committing the offense. The determination of a defendant's role is made on the basis of all conduct within the scope of relevant conduct section of the Guidelines. Several categories applicable to computer crime are given below.

Abuse of Trust or Use of Special Skill

If the defendant abused a position of public or private trust, or used a special skill, in a manner that significantly facilitated the commission or concealment of the offense, increase by two levels. Public or private trust refers to a position of trust characterized by professional or managerial discretion.

"Special skill" refers to a skill not possessed by members of the general public and usually requiring substantial education, training, or licensing. In *U.S. v. Lavin*, the federal appellate court in New York City upheld a district court's imposition of a special skills sentencing enhancement where the defendant had installed electronic equipment in ATMs to obtain PINs and account numbers of bank customers. The court said the defendant used skills that were not possessed by the general public and that these skills greatly facilitated his crime.

Obstruction of Justice

If a defendant willfully obstructs, or attempts to obstruct at any stage of the administration of justice, the offense level is increased by two levels. Obstruction of justice can include a range of actions from making false statements and threatening witnesses, to destruction of evidence.

Groups of Closely Related Counts

All counts involving substantially the same harm are grouped together into a single group. This would cover counts involving the same victim, act, transaction, or conduct. Computer-related fraud comes under this subsection.

DETERMINING THE SENTENCE

Criminal History

A record of a defendant's past criminal conduct, such as number and type of convictions, recidivism, and patterns of career criminal behavior are evaluated and given points to determine the criminal history category in the sentencing table.

Acceptance of Responsibility

If the defendant clearly demonstrates acceptance of responsibility for the offense, decrease the offense level by two levels.

Substantial Assistance to Authorities

Upon motion of the government stating that the defendant has provided substantial assistance in the investigation or prosecution of another person who has committed an offense, the court may depart from the guidelines. "Substantial weight should be given to the government's evaluation of the extent of the defendant's assistance," means essentially that the prosecutor has a big weapon in determining the fate of the defendant.

DETERMINING THE SENTENCE

The defendant's sentence is based on the combined offense level, which is subject to adjustments from the categories discussed above, and from the total points that determine the criminal history category in the sentencing table.

A defendant's record is relevant to sentencing because "a defendant with a record of prior criminal behavior is more culpable than a first offender and thus deserving of greater punishment." Section 4A1.1 of the Guidelines gives items and corresponding points that determine the criminal history category in the sentencing table. Points are tallied for each prior sentence of imprisonment; whether the defendant committed a crime while under any criminal justice sentence; or committed a crime within two years after release from prison; or was convicted for a crime of violence.

Section 4A1.3 covers departures based on how well the criminal history category reflects the seriousness of the defendant's past criminal conduct or the likelihood that the defendant will commit other crimes.

SHOEHORN LAWS: FEDERAL STATUTES USED TO PROSECUTE COMPUTER-RELATED CRIME

A variety of federal laws have been, or could be, used to prosecute computer-related crimes. Several of these laws are very broad and have been used for purposes far beyond their original intent; they are potent legal weapons wielded by the prosecution. The major statutes in the prosecutor's arsenal include conspiracy, mail fraud, wire fraud, the Racketeering and Corrupt Organizations Act (RICO), and the National Stolen Property Act.

CONSPIRACY LAWS

Conspiracy law is relevant to a discussion of computer-related crime, investigation, and litigation because conspiracy violations are often the first things prosecutors look for, as it is generally easier to obtain convictions under these statutes.

The conspiracy statutes have been used in a wide range of cases, limited, it seems, only by the imaginations of prosecutors and litigators. In dealing with a possible computer crime, however, it is wise to be practical and precise, rather than imaginative.

The general federal conspiracy statute says "if two or more persons conspire either to commit any offense against the United States, or to defraud the United States, or any agency thereof in any manner or for any purpose, and one or more of such persons do any act to effect the object of the conspiracy, each shall be fined not more than $10,000 or imprisoned not more than five years or both."[10]

Conspiracy is a group crime, a group agreement, a deliberate plotting to subvert the law. The elements of the crime are:

- The knowing and willful agreement to commit a crime
- Two or more persons
- An action to carry out the conspiracy

---

[10] 18 U.S.C. 371.

Note that the crime of conspiracy is the agreement; this is the critical element. Parties to such illegitimate agreements need not strike a bargain in the traditional business sense—create a written contract, agreement, memo, or have a meeting, etc.—to be prosecuted under the statute. It need only be shown that a person was a party to a conspirational agreement to do something unlawful, during the existence of the conspiracy, what was involved, and was committed to taking part in it to assure its success.

A person involved in a conspiracy is responsible for all that happened during the conspiracy, that is, the acts of each confederate, even though the person may be unaware of their actions.

A member of a conspiracy may get out or withdraw only by doing something to disavow or defeat the purpose of the conspiracy. However, they will remain liable for anything that happened prior to withdrawal.

Evidence

It must be demonstrated that a person had knowledge of the conspiracy, agreed to it, and performed some act to further the conspiracy. Statements and acts of co-conspirators are admissible as evidence if they indicate the above.

Prosecution

To prosecute conspiracy, the offense must be within the court's venue. Usually, conspiracy is merged with another crime since it is normally discovered after a crime has been committed. Therefore, the charges are conspiracy plus a crime. In common law, and some state statutes, the charges are merged. The prosecution must also determine if there is a single conspiracy or multiple conspiracies. A single conspiracy is a single agreement, though it may involve many persons, be complex, and continue over a long period of time.

Prosecutors are aware of the advantages of charging the conspiracy offense, which include the ease of joining charges, the admissibility of co-conspirators' statements, and that it is not necessary to show that each defendant actually committed the offense—only that each agreed to do so.

APPENDIX A

Summary

In an act of conspiracy:

- Two or more persons must agree to commit a criminal act.
- The agreement need only be inferred.
- At least one party to the conspiracy must perform some act in furtherance of the conspiracy (this act need not be criminal).
- One party may be held responsible for the acts of co-conspirators, even though they did not commit any substantive offenses or have actual knowledge of them. A partnership in crime includes all members within its scope and during its time of operation.
- The agreement must be to either violate a criminal statute or, under federal law, to defraud the U.S. government. The definition of fraud is not limited like that of common law. The federal statute includes every conspiracy to impair, obstruct, or defeat any lawful function of the government.

CRIMINAL STATUTES OFTEN MERGED WITH CONSPIRACY

Mail Fraud

The mail fraud statute provides:

> Whoever, having devised or intending to devise any scheme or artifice to defraud, or for obtaining money or property by means of false or fraudulent pretenses, representations, or promises, or to sell, dispose of, loan, exchange, alter, give away, distribute, supply, or furnish or procure for unlawful use any counterfeit or spurious coin, obligation, security, or other article, or anything represented to be or intimated or held out to be such counterfeit or spurious article, for the purpose of executing such scheme or artifice or attempting to do so, places in any post office or authorized depository for mail matter, any matter or thing whatever to be sent or delivered by the postal service or takes or receives therefrom, any such matter or thing, or knowingly causes to be delivered by mail according to the direction thereon, or at the place at which it is directed to be delivered by the person to whom it is addressed, any such matter or thing, shall be fined not more than $1,000 or imprisoned not more than five years, or both.[11]

---

[11] 18 U.S.C. 1341.

Wire Fraud

The essential elements of wire fraud are the devising of a scheme and artifice to defraud and a transmittal in interstate or foreign commerce by means of wire, radio or television communication of writings, signs, signals, pictures, or sounds for the purpose of executing the scheme and artifice to defraud. Here is where transmission of computer data over telephone lines fits. The statute provides:

> Whoever, having devised or intending to devise any scheme or artifice to defraud, or for obtaining money or property by means of false or fraudulent pretenses, representations or promises, transmits or causes to be transmitted by means of wire, radio, or television communication in interstate or foreign commerce, any writings, signs, signals, pictures, or sounds for the purpose of executing such scheme or artifice, shall be fined not more than $1,000 or imprisoned not more than five years, or both.[12]

THE FEDERAL ANTI-RACKETEERING LAW

The federal anti-racketeering law, better known as the RICO (Racketeer Influenced and Corrupt Organizations) Act, has become one of the main legal weapons against a host of crimes.

Key Provisions of the RICO Statutes

RICO does have important application to fraud and computer crime cases. To understand the statutes, one must be cognizant of two key phrases and terms:

- Enterprise . . . Section 1961(4) defines this as any individual, partnership, corporation, association, or other legal entity, any union or group of individuals associated in fact although not a legal entity.
- Pattern of racketeering activity . . . encompasses both the act and the pattern of racketeering. The act of racketeering is defined by those statutes, state and federal, that are mostly broken in organized crime activity; the statute enumerates 32 such offenses.

---

[12] 18 U.S.C. 1343.

APPENDIX A

Convictions Under RICO

At least two of the above acts of racketeering (to form a pattern) must have a nexus, or connection, with the enterprise itself. Thus, for the government to convict under RICO, it must prove both the existence of an enterprise and the connected pattern of racketeering activity. Of the two acts of racketeering, the most recent must have occurred within five years of the indictment, and another within ten years of the most recent act.

Penalties Under RICO

RICO provides both criminal penalties and civil remedies. Criminal penalties are 20 years imprisonment, a $25,000 fine, and forfeiture to the government of any interest in, or property in contractual right to, any enterprise acquired in violation of Section 1962.

Civil remedies in RICO are similar to anti-trust law. In addition, any person injured by the enterprise may sue and recover three times the damage sustained plus court costs and reasonable attorney's fees.

Conclusion

RICO, criminal and civil, is a potent weapon in the prosecution's arsenal. RICO is a complex law with harsh criminal penalties and expansive civil remedies. It is also a law with provisions that could be clarified or limited by the higher courts.

Conspiracy laws should be discussed with legal counsel at the outset of any fraud or computer fraud-related incident that might involve a violation of law. Issues of evidence-gathering, discovery, merged or underlying offenses, or recovery of damages should all be thoroughly examined prior to an investigation or filing of legal charges.

THE LEGAL DEFINITION OF EMBEZZLEMENT

Embezzlement is the fraudulent appropriation of property by a person to whom it has been entrusted, or to whose possession it has lawfully come. It implies a breach of trust or fiduciary responsibility.

THE LEGAL DEFINITION OF EMBEZZLEMENT

Larceny, a closely related offense, is usually defined as the wrongful taking and carrying away of the personal property of another with intent to convert it or to deprive the owner of its use and possession. If the taking is by stealth, the crime committed is larceny. If the taking is by guile and deception, by false representation, or by concealment of that which should have been disclosed, the crime charged may be fraud. The major distinction between larceny and embezzlement lies in the issue of the legality of custody of the article stolen. In larceny, the thief never had legal custody. They "feloniously took" the article stolen. In embezzlement, the thief is legally authorized by the owner to take or receive the article and to possess it for a time. The formulation of intent to steal the article may occur subsequent to the time when it came into his possession or concurrently with initial possession. If initial possession and intent to steal occur simultaneously, the crime is larceny. If intent to steal occurs subsequent to initial possession, the crime is embezzlement. The essence of embezzlement then, lies in the breach of a fiduciary relationship deriving from the entrustment of money.

Federal Statutes on Embezzlement

There are seventy federal criminal statutes covering elements of embezzlement—from labor unions, federal funds to local agencies, commodity exchanges, plus a broad range of federal property.

Most prosecutions occur under the following criminal statutes:

- 18 U.S.C. 641. Covers larceny, embezzlement, or conversion of public monies or property of the United States.
- 18 U.S.C. 656. Covers theft, embezzlement, or misapplication of the bank's money, funds, or credit willfully by an [officer, employee, or others connected to the bank] with intent to injure or defraud a national bank, federally insured bank, or branch or agency of a foreign bank. Sec. 657 covers lending, credit, and insurance institutions.
- 18 U.S.C. 1344. Covers financial institution fraud, scheme, or artifice to defraud a federally insured institution to take money, funds, credits, assets, securities, or other property by misrepresentation.

APPENDIX A

EXTORTION

A broad legal definition of extortion is to obtain money or valuables from a person by violence, threat, or abuse of authority. Most state statutes require the following elements of cause to be shown:

- Oral or written communication
- That the communication maliciously threatens to accuse another of any crime or offense or threaten any injury to the person or property of another
- The intent to extort money or any pecuniary advantage or to compel the victim to do or not to do some act

Usually, there need be no intent of ill will against the victim. Vague threats are insufficient to meet statutory requirements, as are those threats that are not terrifying to the ordinary person. The threat is not dependent on the state of mind of the victim.

In extortion, only the act of extortion itself must be proven. Extortion, however, is one of the most difficult crimes to prosecute successfully because it is often difficult to prove. The extortion threat may be subtly stated or hinted or it may be given to the victim verbally, without witnesses.

Under Federal Codes, the following elements must be proven for criminal conviction:

- Violation to transmit in interstate commerce any message containing any demand or request for ransom or reward for the release of any kidnapped person
- Violation for anyone, who with intent to extort from any person, firm, association, or corporation, money, or any thing of value which threat is transmitted in interstate commerce and threatens to kidnap any person or threaten to harm another

FORGERY

An embezzlement often involves forged documents and the law of forgery (the material altering of a document with the intent to defraud) comes into play. Forgery may also be the entry of false passwords into a computer to gain access and use the computer to defraud.

MONEY LAUNDERING

The Money Laundering Control Act of 1986 (18 USC 1956-1957) was passed in October 1986 as part of the Anti-Drug Abuse Act of 1986. The Act created two new offenses related to money laundering and currency transaction reporting violations. Reporting requirements are required for parties engaged in certain cash transactions, and money-laundering violations are now predicate acts under RICO.

FORFEITURE STATUTES

Forfeiture statutes are either criminal or civil in nature. A criminal forfeiture is litigated in the trial that determines the defendant's guilt and is ordered only after the defendant-violator is found guilty. Since other parties who may have an interest in the forfeitable property cannot participate in the criminal trial, a verdict of forfeiture settles title in favor of the government only as against the criminal defendant. Post-trial hearings must be held in order to allow third-party claimants to defend their interests in the property.

Conversely, a civil forfeiture is not an action against an individual but an action against the property itself. Civil forfeiture proceedings can be completed before a criminal defendant is charged or convicted, after the defendant's acquittal, or even absent any criminal charge. Unlike criminal forfeiture actions where the government must prove the forfeitable offense beyond a reasonable doubt, the burden of proof in civil forfeiture actions shifts to the claimant once the government has established probable cause to sustain the forfeiture. A civil forfeiture action settles the government's title to the property as against the world. No further proceedings relating to property title are necessary.

STATE COMPUTER CRIME STATUTES

State statutes tend either to be comprehensive or deal exclusively with computer-related crime by defining specific computer elements and offensive acts. Alternatively, computer-related offenses may be merged with existing statutes covering established crimes.

Crimes involving computers have and continue to be prosecuted using "shoehorn" laws such as embezzlement, larceny, malicious mischief, and fraud. In the federal courts, mail or wire fraud, interstate transportation of stolen property, and conspiracy statutes are commonly used. However, many legislatures felt the need for an additional statute that proscribed various forms of computer abuse.

STATE COMPUTER CRIME
STATUTES AND CODE LOCATION

Alabama	Ala. Code 13A-8-101 to 103
Alaska	Alas. Stat. sec. 11.46.200(a) and 11.46.740
Arizona	Ariz. Rev. Stat. sec. 13-2316
Arkansas	Ark. Stat. sec. 5-41-101 to 107
California	Cal. Penal Code sec. 502
Colorado	Colo. Rev. Stat. sec. 18-5.5-101 to 102
Connecticut	Conn. Gen. Stat. Ann. sec. 53a-250 to 261
Delaware	Del. Code tit. 11, sec. 931-939
Florida	Fla. Stat. Ann. sec. 815.01 to 815.07
Georgia	Ga. Code Ann. sec. 16-9-90 to 95
Hawaii	Haw. Rev. Stat. 708-890 to 896
Idaho	Idaho Code sec. 18-2201 to 2202
Illinois	Ill. Stat. Ann. ch. 38, sec. 16D to 7
Indiana	IC 35-43-1-4 and 35-43-2-3
Iowa	Iowa Code Ann. sec. 716A.1 to 16
Kansas	Kans. Stat. sec. 21-3755
Kentucky	Ky. Rev. Stat. sec. 434.840 to 860
Louisiana	La. Rev. Stat. 14:73.1 through 5
Maine	Me. Rev. Stat. Ann. tit. 17-A sec. 431-433
Maryland	Md. Ann. Code Art. 27, sec. 146
Massachusetts	Mass. Gen Laws Ann. ch. 266, sec. 30(2)
Michigan	Mich. Comp. Laws Ann. sec. 752.791 to 797
Minnesota	Minn. Stat. Ann. sec. 609.87 to 891
Mississippi	Miss. Code Ann. sec. 97-45-1 to 13
Missouri	Mo. Ann. Stat. sec. 569.093 to 099
Montana	Mont. Code Ann. 45-6-310 to 311
Nebraska	Neb. Rev. Stat. sec. 28-1343 to 1348
Nevada	Nev. Rev. Stat. sec. 205.473 to 490
New Hampshire	N.H. Rev. Stat. Ann. sec. 638:16 to 19

New Jersey	N.J. Rev. Stat. sec. 2C:20-23 to 34
New Mexico	N.M. Stat. Ann. sec. 30-45-1 to 7
New York	N.Y. Penal Law Art. 156 to 156.50
North Carolina	N.C. Gen. Stat. 14-453 to 457
North Dakota	N.D. Cent. Code sec. 12.1-06.1-08
Ohio	Ohio Rev. Code Ann. sec. 2913.014
Oklahoma	Okla. Stat. Ann. tit. 21, sec. 1951–1958
Oregon	Or. Rev. Stat. 164.377
Pennsylvania	Pa. Stat. Ann. tit. 18, sec. 3933
Rhode Island	R.I. Gen. Laws sec. 11-52-2 to 5
South Carolina	S.C. Code sec. 16-16-10 to 40
South Dakota	S.D. Codified Laws Ann. sec. 43-43B-1 to 8
Tennessee	Tenn. Code Ann. sec. 39-14-601 to 603
Texas	Tex. Penal Code sec. 33.01-33.05
Utah	Utah Code Ann. sec. 76-6-701 to 705
Virginia	Va. Code Ann. sec. 18.2-152.1 to 14
Washington	Wash. Rev. Code Ann. sec. 9A.52.110 to 130
West Virginia	W.Va. Code sec. 61-3c-1 to 21
Wisconsin	Wis. Stat. Ann. sec. 943.70
Wyoming	Wyo. Stat. sec. 6-3-501 to 505
Utah	Utah Code Ann. sec. 76-6-701

APPENDIX B

INTELLECTUAL PROPERTY LAW

TRADE SECRETS LAW

Technological and business information that is used secretly within an enterprise, which lends a competitive advantage, and which is not known generally by competitors, is legally protectable as a trade secret. Matter protectable as a trade secret is broad and includes varieties of information for which patent protection is never available. For many types of technological information, such as complex industrial processes and formulas, trade secrets and patents are alternative forms of protection. Other innovative matter, such as computer software and related developments, which may be marginally protectable by patent or copyright, are better protected as trade secrets.

Trade secret law has been ruled by the Supreme Court to be independent of and complimentary with the patent system. This allows, for example, the choice of either seeking patent protection for computer software or retaining the matter as a trade secret. (See *Gottschalk v. Benson,* 409 U.S. 63 [1972])

Trade secret law is generally based on common law and contractual provisions. While patent and copyright are under federal law, the law of each state defines what a trade secret is, the right of the holder, and the enforcement of all trade secret claims. State trade secret law is not pre-empted by federal law and unlike patent or copyright, there is no limit on the duration of a trade secret.

A federal statute, the Trade Secrets Act, 18 U.S.C. 1905, prohibits unauthorized release of any information relating to trade secrets or confidential business information by a federal officer or employee.

ELEMENTS OF TRADE SECRETS LAW

For confidential information to be given the status of a trade secret it must be commercial information. That is, it cannot be just any information that a firm does not want known, such as an internal report that discloses poor management practices. The commercial information must have a value that lies in the competitive advantage it gives over business rivals. Another essential element of a trade secret is its confidential nature, which must be maintained.

In 1979 the Uniform Trade Secrets Act (UTSA) was approved by the National Conference of Commissioners on Uniform State Laws and amended in 1985. UTSA, which has been adopted, with variations, into the civil codes of over 30 states, gives the following definition of a trade secret:

Trade secret means information, including a formula, pattern, compilation, program, device, method, technique, or process that:

1. Derives independent economic value, actual or potential, from not being generally known to, and not being readily ascertainable by proper means, by other persons who can obtain economic value from its disclosure or use

2. Is the subject of efforts that are reasonable under the circumstances to maintain its secrecy.

ECONOMIC ESPIONAGE ACT

The Economic Espionage Act of 1996 (Public Law 104-294) is designed to protect proprietary economic information. It creates criminal penalties for the theft, unauthorized appropriation or conversion, duplication, alteration, destruction, wrongful copying or control of trade secrets, or the wrongful diversion of a trade secret to the economic benefit of someone other than its owners, or some disadvantage to the rightful owners.

The Act amends Title 18 of the U.S. Code by inserting a new chapter, 90. Section 1831 of the chapter prohibits anyone from obtaining trade secrets by fraud, theft, or deception for the benefit of a foreign agent or government. Individuals can be fined up to $500,000 and imprisoned up to 15 years. Organizations can be fined up to $10 million.

The term *wrongful* involves "the defendant's knowledge that his or her actions in copying or otherwise exerting control over the information in question was inappropriate. It is not necessary that the government prove that the defendant knew his or her actions were illegal, rather the government must prove that the defendant's actions were not authorized by the nature of his or her relationship to the owner of the property and that the defendant knew or should have known that fact."[1] Under the Act, the government must prove the defendant acted "the intent to, or with reason to believe that the offense would, benefit any foreign government, foreign instrumentality, or foreign agent."

The Act calls for a broad definition of *benefit* that goes beyond a strictly economic advantage that can also confer a reputational, strategic, or tactical benefit.

The Act seeks to get at methods of misappropriation or destruction that involve duplication or alteration. "When these non-traditional methods are used, the original property never leaves the control of the rightful owner, but the unauthorized duplication or misappropriation effectively destroys the value of what is left with the rightful owner."[2] With computer systems, information can be stolen without being "carried off" as defined in traditional theft statutes. "It is the intent of this statute to ensure that the theft of intangible information is prohibited in the same way that the theft of physical items is punished."[3]

Receiving, buying, or possessing a trade secret known to be stolen is an offense. Attempts to steal, or conspiracies to steal, trade secrets are also prohibited. A trade secret is defined as "all forms and types of financial, business, scientific, technical, economic, or engineering information,"[4] having independent economic value, and for which the owner has "taken reasonable measures to keep such information secret."[5] A determination of the "reasonableness of the steps taken by the owner to keep the information secret will vary from case to case and be dependent upon the nature of the information in question."[6]

Congress intended this Act to help federal law enforcement combat trade secret thefts by foreign companies, often with the cooperation of foreign governments, and thefts by U.S. employees. Also, there is no federal criminal statute that deals directly with

---

[1-6] Public Law 104-294. The Economic Espionage Act.

economic espionage or the protection of proprietary economic information. Under existing law, there is no statutory procedure to protect the victim's stolen information during criminal proceedings. In any prosecution or proceeding, the court may issue orders to preserve the confidentiality of trade secrets. In a civil action, the Attorney General may issue injunctive relief against any violation under this act.

Under Section 1832, it is an offense to convert a trade secret that is related to or a part of a product in interstate or foreign commerce, where the trade secret was obtained without authorization or through theft. It is also unlawful for anyone, without authorization from the owner, to make copies of trade secret information, or communicate such information, or to receive or buy, or to attempt or conspire to do any of the above that would cause injury to the trade secret owner. Conviction carries a fine or imprisonment of not more than ten years or both. Organizations can be fined not more than five million dollars.

The statute includes a criminal forfeiture provision in addition to any other sentence. Any property or proceeds derived from the crime, or property used or intended to be used in the crime, may be forfeited.

Tort Law Protection for Trade Secrets

A trade secret takes on the attribute of property to be protected, as another asset of the firm. In the Restatement of Torts, Section 757, we find further clarification of factors to be considered in determining whether information can be a secret:

- The extent to which the information is known outside of the business
- The extent to which it is known by employees and others involved in the business
- The extent of measures taken by the business to guard the secrecy of the information
- The value of the information to the business and its competitors
- The amount of effort or money expended by the business in developing the information
- The ease or difficulty with which the information could be properly acquired or duplicated by others

To establish a claim of misappropriation of a trade secret, the Restatement says:

- There must be a protectable interest (i.e., a trade secret).
- The plaintiff must have a proprietary interest in the trade secret.
- The trade secret must be disclosed to the defendant in confidence or it must be wrongfully acquired by the defendant through improper means.
- There must be a duty not to use or disclose the information.
- There must be a likely or past disclosure or use of the information, if in a different form, which is unfair or inequitable to the plaintiff.

The Concept of Novelty

To be protected as a trade secret, the information must be novel. It cannot exist in the public domain. However, the information could be combined in such a way to make it new and uniquely different and possibly qualify for trade secret protection.

Information that could be a candidate for trade secret status is often created and stored on a computer. Take, for example, market research data. As it is collected in raw data, such as survey questionnaire tabulations, it may not meet the requirements of a trade secret but it would certainly justify being protected as proprietary information. However, the methodology used, say a proprietary survey sampling technique, or the mailing list, if it was compiled in-house using customer names, should qualify as a trade secret.

Then again, all of the elements used in a marketing research survey—the research methodology, the survey select sample, and the statistical analysis—may be commonly known. Yet, the combination of these elements can result in marketing information or a plan that qualifies as a trade secret.

Two elements are now present: unique, novel information not in the public domain, and information that confers a commercially competitive advantage, or potential advantage, to its owner. The novelty of the plan or one of its elements is not necessarily critical to trade secret status; it is the totality of the plan that is unique in that everything about it is not common industry knowledge, and that the marketing plan confers a competitive advantage.

APPENDIX B

How Trade Secrets Can Lose Their Confidentiality

Proper means to discover a trade secret include:

- Independent invention
- Reverse engineering
- Observation of the item in public use or on public display
- Obtaining the information from public literature

The clearest way to abandon secrecy is to make public disclosure of the information. This does not necessarily mean broad public dissemination; a single third party will suffice as long as it is made in the absence of confidential circumstances. A patent issuance will end trade secret status. The age or relevance of the information can also affect its trade secret status.

The legal interpretation of the phrase "reasonable under the circumstances," with regard to safeguarding trade secrets has varied in the courts. In several cases, the courts have held that security need only comprise reasonable efforts. In a 1970 case, *E.I. duPont de Nemours & Co. v. Christopher*, the court ruled that :

> "We should not require a person or corporation to take unreasonable precautions to prevent another from doing that which he ought not to do in the first place. Reasonable precautions against predatory eyes we may require, but an impenetrable fortress is an unreasonable requirement."

In a 1991 case, *Rockwell Graphics Systems v. DEV Industries, Inc.*, Rockwell Graphics accused DEV of misappropriating valuable design drawings. DEV countered by arguing that the drawings had been obtained lawfully and that Rockwell had given up its right to trade secret protection because the drawings were widely circulated to independent machine shops and because the company had not taken reasonable security measures to guard their secrecy. Rockwell said it had confidentiality agreements with the independent machine shops and that the cost of maintaining secrecy should not be unreasonable.

Rockwell also filed a federal RICO (Racketeering Influenced and Corrupt Organizations) lawsuit against DEV.

The case went to the U.S. Court of Appeals in Chicago after a federal district court agreed with DEV. Judge Richard Posner, writing for the Appeals Court which reversed the District Court's verdict, said:

> "This is an important case because trade secret protection is an important part of intellectual property, a form of property that is of growing importance to the competitiveness of American industry . . . If trade secrets are protected only if their owners take extravagant, productivity-impairing measures to maintain their secrecy, the incentive to invest resources in discovering more efficient methods of production will be reduced, and with it the amount of invention."

Posner said the courts should balance the costs of maintaining secrecy against its benefits in determining whether a company's security practices were reasonable enough to justify trade secret protections.

On the other hand, more than just good intentions and a show of security are necessary to claim adequate protection was afforded confidential information. The courts will look at each case involving misappropriation of alleged trade secrets and make a determination as to the effectiveness of security.

The courts have given guidance on misappropriating a trade secret. The statutory definition says that no person, including the state, may misappropriate or threaten to misappropriate a trade secret by:

- Acquiring the trade secret of another by means which the person knows or has reason to know constitute improper means
- Disclosing or using without express or implied consent a trade secret of another if the person used improper means to acquire knowledge of the trade secret; or if, at the time of disclosure or use, the person knew or had reason to know that he or she obtained knowledge of the trade secret through any of the following means:
  - Deriving it from or through a person who utilized improper means to acquire it
  - Acquiring it under circumstances giving rise to a duty to maintain its secrecy or limit its use

- Deriving it from or through a person who owed a duty to the person seeking relief to maintain its secrecy or limit its use
- Acquiring it by accident or mistake

The phrase *improper means* has been defined to include espionage, theft, bribery, misrepresentation, and breach or inducement of a breach of duty to maintain secrecy.

REMEDIES FOR MISAPPROPRIATION OF TRADE SECRETS

Criminal Prosecution

State statutes covering trade secret theft usually contain criminal sanctions.

INJUNCTIVE REMEDIES

As soon as a trade secret misappropriation is discovered, the quickest legal tactic is to ask the court for a temporary restraining order or preliminary injunction. This forces the offender to immediately cease violating a confidentiality agreement.

You need to be ready to show the court the value of the information and the damage the enterprise will suffer if the trade secret information is disseminated or misused.

Recovery for Damages

For trade secret misappropriation by employees compensatory damages can be recovered. In determining damages, the court may examine the trade secret owner's loss or the defendant's gain, or both. Here again, knowing the fact of damage caused by the loss of a trade secret is the critical first step; the next step is to determine and show the amount of damages.

Punitive damages may also be awarded if the defendant's conduct was willful and malicious misappropriation of the owner's trade secret.

NATIONAL STOLEN PROPERTY ACT

The National Stolen Property Act calls for criminal sanctions against any person who "transports, transmits, or transfers in interstate or foreign commerce any goods, wares, merchandise, securities or money, of the value of $5,000 or more, knowing the same to have been stolen, converted or taken by fraud . . ."[7] Penalties can be a fine of up to $10,000 or a prison sentence of ten years or both.

Federal courts have ruled that confidential information stored on a computer was valuable property under the definition of "goods, wares, or merchandise"; and a person who "transmitted" stolen proprietary business information from one computer to another across state lines could be prosecuted under the statute.

The key clauses of the statute that must be satisfied for a conviction are:

- The items must be transported or transmitted in interstate or foreign commerce.
- The items must meet the definition of goods, wares, merchandise, securities, or money.
- The items—property or money—must have a value of $5,000 or more.
- The defendant must have knowledge that the items were stolen or falsely made.
- The items must have been stolen, converted or taken by fraudulent means.

The aim of the statute is to prohibit the use of interstate transportation facilities to move stolen goods and to punish theft of property that was beyond the capability of an individual state. Therefore, the movement of a trade secret across state lines must be established. Also, it must be established that the defendant had knowledge that the information was property and that it was stolen.

Obviously, other federal laws come into play when stolen information is transferred or transmitted. First are the wire or mail fraud statutes; these statutes are often merged with or underlay a charge of conspiracy.

---

[7] 18 U.S.C. Sec. 2314. The National Stolen Property Act.

INTERNATIONAL PROTECTIONS FOR TRADE SECRETS

Protection of trade secrets (called undisclosed information) in all GATT (General Agreement on Tariffs or Trade) countries is covered in Article 39. Natural as well as legal persons may prevent information being disclosed to, acquired by, or used by others without their consent so long as the information is relatively secret, has commercial value because it is secret, and has been the subject of reasonable efforts to keep the information secret.

NAFTA (North American Free Trade Alliance) uses the broader phrase "actual or potential" commercial value. (17, Article 1711 (1)(b))

A gross negligence standard is established for disclosure of trade secrets to third parties.

COPYRIGHT LAW

The Copyright Act of 1976 is a revision of the Copyright Act of 1909; U.S.C. Title 17 became fully effective on January 1, 1978.

In 1980, copyright legislation extended protection to computer programs (17 USC 107, 117). Computer programs are copyrightable as "literary works."

To come under copyright protection, a work must be:

- In the form of a "writing," that is, fixed in any tangible medium of expression now known or later developed, from which they can be perceived, reproduced, or otherwise communicated, either directly or with the aid of a machine or device.
- A product of original creative authorship.

If a work does not display a copyright notice, that does not mean the work is not copyrighted. Although federal registration is not required to have a valid copyright, registration is necessary for federal court jurisdiction and for obtaining statutory damages.

Computer programs or software fall under copyrightable works. The definition of "literary works" refers to works expressed in "words, numbers, or other verbal or numerical symbols or indicia."[8] A computer program is defined in section 101 as "a set of statements

---

[8] Copyright Act of 1976. Section 101.

or instructions used directly or indirectly in a computer in order to bring about a certain result." It should be noted that only the programmer's "literary" expression (i.e., the program) would be copyrightable, not any "procedure, process, system, method of operation, concept, principle, or discovery, regardless of the form in which it is described, explained, illustrated, or embodied."[9]

Copyright grants the owner the exclusive right to do and to authorize others to:

- Reproduce copies of the copyrighted work
- Prepare derivative works based on the copyrighted work
- Distribute copies of the copyrighted work to the public by sale or other transfer of ownership, or by rental, lease, or lending
- Perform the copyrighted work publicly
- Display the copyrighted work publicly (17 USC 106)

Infringement of Copyright and Criminal Acts

It is an infringement of the copyright for anyone to engage in any of the activities listed above without the authorization of the copyright owner.

Under copyright law there are four kinds of criminal acts:

1. Infringement of "a copyright willfully and for purposes of commercial advantage or private financial gain"

2. Intentional fraudulent uses of copyright notice whereby copyright notice is placed on an article when the defendant knows the notice to be false

3. Fraudulent removal of copyright notice

4. Knowingly making a false representation in a copyright registration application

Criminal copyright can also arise from the distribution of infringing goods.

In a criminal prosecution for copyright infringement the government must prove: that a copyright was infringed; that it was a willful violation; and that the infringement was for profit.

---

[9] Copyright Act of 1976. Section 102(b).

CRIMINAL AND CIVIL PENALTIES

The 1992 amendments to the Copyright Act stiffened criminal penalties: convicted first offenders may get prison sentences for up to five years or fines of up to $250,000 for individuals, $500,000 for an organization. With a previous conviction, the maximum prison sentence could be ten years.

A forfeiture clause allows the courts to seize and destroy infringing items plus "all implements, devices or equipment used in the manufacture of . . . infringing copies."[10]

FAIR USE DOCTRINE

Our copyright system is based on the dual interests of property rights and intellectual promotion. Fair use makes the copyright law flexible, rather than a rigid doctrine; it does not impede or stifle creative activity.

Congress codified the doctrine of fair use in the 1976 Copyright Act; however, it did not define the term, leaving its interpretation to the courts. Section 107 of the Copyright Act gives four factors that courts may consider in deciding whether a particular use is fair:

1. The purpose and character of the use, including whether such use is of a commercial nature or is for nonprofit educational purposes

2. The nature of the copyrighted work

3. The amount and substantiality of the portion used in relation to the copyrighted work as a whole

4. The effect of the use upon the potential market for or the value of the copyrighted work.

Congress has expressed that the above four factors are neither all-inclusive nor determinative but can provide "some gauge for balancing equities." These factors, therefore, are a flexible set of guidelines for the courts to use in analyzing and deciding each individual copyright infringement case where the issue is one of fair use.

---

[10] Copyright Act of 1976. 1992 Amendments.

Courts must evaluate whether the use of copyrighted material was of a commercial nature or for a nonprofit educational, scientific, or historical purpose; whether the nature of the copyrighted work was published in a tangible form or was unpublished material. What amount, in quantity, and substantiality—its core or essence—of the work was used? Did the defendant's alleged conduct have an adverse effect on the potential market or value of the copyrighted work.

THE PREEMPTION CLAUSE

The first Copyright Act of 1790 gave the United States a dual system of copyright: federal law protected published works; common law or state law protected the body of unpublished works. The Copyright Act of 1909 preserved the common law right of authors in their unpublished works. The Copyright Act of 1976 ended this dual system by attaching federal copyright protection to a work the moment it is fixed in tangible form. The federal government was also given complete responsibility for enforcing copyright law.

Congress could have looked to the Supremacy Clause of the Constitution (Article VI, clause 2) to end the dual system of federal and state law, but instead chose to legislate explicitly on preemption.

The key provision on preemption is Section 301 of the Act of 1976 that ends copyright protections under the common law or statutes of any state.

In the House Report on the 1976 Copyright bill, the intention of section 301 is "to preempt and abolish any rights under the common law or statutes of a state that are equivalent to copyright and extend to works coming within the scope of the federal copyright law. The declaration of this principle in section 301 is intended to be stated in the clearest and most unequivocal language possible, so as to foreclose any conceivable misinterpretation of its unqualified intention that Congress shall act preemptively, and to avoid the development of any vague borderline areas between state and federal protection."[11]

Title 28 USC, Section 1338 makes it clear that any action involving rights under the federal copyright law come within the exclusive jurisdiction of the federal courts.

---

[11] Copyright Act of 1976, House Report.

APPENDIX B

For a state law to be preempted, two conditions must be met:

1. The state right must be "equivalent to any of the exclusive rights within the general scope of copyright as specified by section 106."

2. The right must be "in works of authorship that are fixed in a tangible medium of expression and come within the subject matter of copyright as specified by sections 102 and 103." (See above)

Two general areas are left unaffected by the preemption:

1. Subject matter that does not come within the subject matter of copyright

2. Violations of rights that are not equivalent to any of the exclusive rights under copyright

The House Report gives examples of actions and rights which are not preempted and differ from copyright, including misappropriation, as long as it "is in fact based neither on a right within the general scope of copyright as specified by section 106 nor on a right equivalent thereto." The 1976 Act, in effect, "preserved rights under state law with respect to activities violating rights that are not equivalent to any of the exclusive rights within the general scope of copyright," including misappropriation, trespass, conversion, breaches of contract or trust, defamation, invasion of privacy, deceptive trade practices, breaching the security of a computer database, and electronic interception of data.

States may not add an additional element that creates a distinguishable offense from the proscriptions in the Copyright Act to their criminal statutes.

State computer crime laws may be in violation of the U.S. Constitution and preempted if property is defined to include copyrighted information, or criminal acts that involve copyright material. Cases in state courts could be dismissed.

The alternative, of course, is to file possible criminal copyright infringements in federal courts under the Copyright Act. As discussed above, the federal criminal and civil penalties are harsh. Before bringing any case to a federal attorney, you must know precisely what has been infringed, have specific allegations, and even some solid evidence. The Feds do not have a lot of resources—training, manpower, and expertise—in intellectual property law violations or prosecutions. Be prepared to do your own investigation. Examine your state's computer crime law and look at other statutes covering theft, conversion, and conspiracy.

SAFE HARBORS FOR SERVICE PROVIDERS

The Digital Millennium Copyright Act (DMCA), 17 USC Sec. 512, enacted in 1998, offers four safe harbors to online service providers (SPs). One safe harbor applies to SPs if a third party initiated the transmission of infringed material, if the functions were carried automatically, and if a copy was retained only long enough to perform the transmission function.

Another safe harbor applies to caching or temporary storage of material on the network. Another applies to storage a user requested. A safe harbor is also given to an SP when a user links to a site with infringing material, if there is no actual knowledge the site is infringing.

The DCMA also prohibits the circumvention of technical methods that control access to a copyrighted work. The DCMA implements the World Intellectual Copyright Organization (WIPO) copyright treaty of 1996.

WEB PAGE VANDALISM: SOME SUGGESTED LEGAL PROTECTION

The Computer Fraud and Abuse Act (Title 18 U.S.C., Section 1030) is the broad federal source for computer legal protection. Section 1030(a)(5) defines any "protected computer" to include government computers, financial institution computers, and any computer used in interstate or foreign commerce or communications. The Act criminalizes any intentional act of trespass and all damage to a computer.

State and federal malicious mischief statutes are another legal weapon against computer vandalism. For instance, under USC 18, Section 1361, malicious mischief comprises "whoever willfully injures or commits any depredation against any property of the

United States, or any department or agency thereof, or any property which has been or is being manufactured or constructed for the United States, or any department or agency thereof . . ."

Section 1362 covers malicious injury to communications lines, stations or systems, "or other means of communication, operated or controlled by the United States . . ." or "maliciously interferes in any way with the working or use of any such line, or system . . . or obstructs, hinders or delays the transmission of any communication over any such line, or system."[12]

A legal remedy for malicious acts originally designed for curbing unsolicited advertising via fax that can tie up your system, may lie in the Telephone Consumer Protection Act of 1991 (TCPA) (47 USCS Section 227, and collateral Code of Federal Regulations 47 CFR Section 64.1200). The TCPA defines a fax as the equivalent of E-mail; that is, if your computer has a modem connected to a regular telephone line and a printer connected to that computer. An unsolicited advertising sent via E-mail to a fax is the same. This law might be applied to Internet or Web communications. It could also apply to framing, where essentially advertising is sent when a user clicks onto your website and your ad material is blocked out by the framing.

The TCPA allows a private right of action against the sender of unsolicited advertising, provided the company did not have a prior "established business relationship" with the sender. The recipient can sue for $500 for each violation, or actual monetary loss. Whichever sum is greater may determine the tactic, but the recipient may sue for both the violation penalty and the sum lost. An injunction action is also available. If the court finds the defendant willfully or knowingly violated the TCPA, the court has the discretion of tripling the damage award.

The TCPA defines unsolicited advertising as "any material advertising the commercially availability or quality of any property goods or services which is transmitted . . ."

Congress has stated that the purpose of the TCPA is to facilitate interstate commerce. The TCPA was felt to be consistent with the First Amendment as it does not restrict or discriminate messages based on their content; it regulates and restricts only the manner and place.

---

[12] Title 18 U.S.C., Section 1362. The Computer Fraud and Abuse Act.

TRADEMARKS

The Federal Trademark Statute

The Lanham Trademark Act of 1946 (15 U.S.C. Sec. 1051-1127, 1988 ed. and Supp. V) gives a seller or producer the exclusive right to register a trademark and to prevent competitors from using that trademark. Registration is in effect for 10 years; an affidavit of continued use must be filed in the sixth year. Renewal can occur any number of successive 10-year terms so long as the mark is still in commercial use. The trademark must be used in interstate commerce, although federal protection may still apply if the trademark has an affect on interstate commerce. Establishing a Web page for access to all users satisfies the Lanham Act's "in commerce" requirement.

A producer may apply for a trademark if there is an "intent to use" the mark; the use must occur in six months or an extension can be requested. The Lanham Act says that trademarks "include any word, name, symbol, or device, or any combination thereof. A symbol or device may be almost anything that can carry meaning.

Trade Dress

Until recently, trade dress protection basically meant original packaging; now it refers to a product's total image. Competitors can therefore be stopped from imitating the general appearance or image of a product or service if the trade dress was either inherently distinctive or had acquired a secondary meaning.

Trademark Dilution

The Federal Trademark Dilution Act of 1995 (Public Law 104-98) is aimed at protecting famous marks and allows injunctive action against a party that causes dilution of the distinctive quality of the mark. Dilution is defined as "the lessening of the capacity of a mark to identify and distinguish goods or services, regardless of the presence or absence of (1) competition between the owner of the famous mark and other parties, or (2) likelihood of confusion, mistake, or deception."[13]

---

[13] Public Law 109-98. The Federal Trademark Dilution Act of 1945.

Other legal action can be taken if it can be proven that the "person against whom the injunction is sought willfully intended to trade on the owner's reputation or to cause dilution of the famous mark." It will be up to the court to determine damages, which could include triple damages.

Naming Websites: Domain Names

A domain name distinguishes a commercial site on the Internet by providing a unique name and address. On the far right of a domain name is a standard abbreviation representing the type of entity, such as ".com" for commercial, ".edu" for educational institutions, and ".gov" for government entities. To the left of the type of entity is a unique domain name; left of this is the user name.

A domain name may function as a trademark and suggest identity, quality, and content of the Internet or Website.

Civil Actions and Sanctions for Trademark Violations

A court-ordered temporary restraining order or an injunction is designed to protect the property of the plaintiff and could be issued to restrain ongoing or future infringing acts. The court must first decide if the party seeking to restrain was more diligent in protecting its property rights than the accused infringer. An injunction can be issued against an organization or its agent, officers, or employees.

Besides an injunction, the court may grant an order for the seizure of goods and counterfeit marks and the means of making such marks and the destruction of all materials and equipment.

In addition to any damages sustained by the plaintiff, the court may order the defendant's profits be given the plaintiff as well as paying the plaintiff's legal costs.

APPENDIX C

CYBERTORT LAWS

The United States has been described as a litigious society, and some lawyers call certain states "tort heaven." These terms describe both an attitude and a fact of life and of doing business. It was announced five years ago that a trial lawyer's association formed two groups, one concentrating on computer vendor liability and the other on inadequate security litigation.

It is not only civil liability risks that are growing. Large and small businesses today are faced with lessened standards of criminal liability and a trend to criminalize regulations that were once essentially civil. Federal legislation initially intended to fight criminal racketeering and narcotics-related crimes has given prosecutors broad powers to indict, compel plea bargaining, and force cooperation of individual or corporation defendants.

Prosecution used to hinge on the concept of intent but this has often been replaced by evidence of "willful blindness," "recklessness," "failure to perceive (a risk)," or "collective knowledge" for corporate liability. Added to these risks could be the expensive prospect of collateral prosecution and litigation, or being twice charged, tried, and possibly fined or sentenced for a single violation. While legal costs can be exorbitant, litigation can also damage a company's reputation, harm employee, customer, and investor relations, and possibly diminish credit lines.

This chapter will examine several of the key legal elements that define liability; specifically, those risks associated with computer protection.

FORESEEABILITY, DUE CARE, AND NEGLIGENCE

"The probability of injury by one to the legally protected interests of another is the basis for the law's creation of a duty to avoid such injury, and foresight of harm lies at the foundation of the duty to use care and therefore of negligence. The broad test of negligence is what a reasonably prudent person would foresee and would do in the light of this foresight under the circumstances."[1] In possible criminal situations, "an actor . . . must anticipate and guard against . . . criminal misconduct of others."[2] Further, it doesn't matter if the consequences of the act are unforeseeable: "the test is not what the wrongdoer believed would occur; it is whether he ought reasonably to have foreseen that the event in question, or some similar event would occur."[3]

While our focus here is on liability risks rising from an absence of or inadequate computer security, we must be aware that legal issues, initially developed in one area, have a way of migrating into totally different fields. Such is the nature of foreseeability and its relationship to negligence and computer security. Liability can also arise from awareness of the imminent probability of specific harm to another.

The legal issue of foreseeability centers on the legal obligation of one party to protect another, second party against foreseeable, intentional wrongs done by a third party. The connection among parties is usually that of a business or a vendor to a customer or client; the wrongful act may be committed by a vandal, thief, etc. Normally, in the past, responsibility or duty of care existed between the business and the customer. The owner was rarely blamed for the acts a criminal inflicted on a customer, even if the act occurred on or near the owner's property.

Increasingly, the courts find a connection between parties, laying negligence on the business/owner for failing to be aware of risks to customers from acts of third parties. The key phrase here is "aware of risks." The owner should be aware of the risks to his customers inherent in his business operations and the surrounding environment. The concept of foreseeability is increasingly used in cases where negligence rests on absent or inadequate security.

RISK AWARENESS

How does one foresee a risk? It is hard to foresee a very specific risk; what matters in law is not that you're clairvoyant, but that you be

---

[1] *American Jurisprudence 2d*, Sect. 135.
[2, 3] *American Jurisprudence 2d*, Sect. 164.

aware of those risks that might affect your customers and that you take appropriate precautions to alleviate those risks.

This, in short, is a definition of the duty of care. But what should your level of knowledge be? What should a reasonable person have known? What is the appropriate set of precautions? How much security should you have?

There is less likelihood of charges of security negligence and greater chances of recovery when appropriate precautions are taken. Remember, appropriate security does not mean just some security (that's likely to be called inadequate), but a well-designed and tested system. This is your best defense against charges of negligence and attendant liability.

Foreseeability should be evaluated in terms of:

- Prior similar incidents, their frequency and recentness
- Whether certain acts were "enhanced" by poor security
- The "totality of the circumstances," that is, the circumstances surrounding the incident

There are no hard and fast rules as to what is legally foreseeable or what is reasonable security. It is situational and must be examined case by case. To give you a better idea of the relationship between foreseeability, security and negligence, the relevant legal concepts are outlined in the sections that follow.

NEGLIGENCE DEFINED

Negligence is related to duty of care and defined by four elements:

1. A legally recognized duty to act as a reasonable person under the circumstances

2. A breach of the duty by failing to live up to the standard

3. A reasonably close causal connection, known as proximate cause which includes cause in fact

4. Actual loss or damages[4]

---

[4] W. Page Keeton et al., Prosser and Keeton on the Law of Torts (5th ed. 1984).

Further, "foresight of harm lies at the foundation of the duty to use care and therefore of negligence. The broad test of negligence is what a reasonably prudent person would foresee and would do in the light of this foresight under the circumstances." [5]

DUTY OF CARE

The duty of care requirement involves:

- Foreseeability of harm to the plaintiff
- Closeness of the connection between the defendant's conduct and the injury incurred
- Degree of injury received
- Moral blame attached to the defendant's conduct
- Policy of preventing future harm

"Duty of care is not sacrosanct in itself, but only an expression of the sum total of those considerations of policy which leads the law to say that the plaintiff is entitled to protection." [6]

NOTICE

Liability can also arise from awareness of the imminent probability of specific harm to another. This is legally referred to as notice, or having specific knowledge concerning the existence of a fact or condition. Notice may give rise to a duty to protect, or at least to investigate the situation.

LIABILITY FOR INADEQUATE SECURITY

Organizations can be held liable for inadequate security if there is evidence that:

- The crime was similar to a previous crime committed on their property.

---

[5] *American Jurisprudence 2d*, Sect. 135.
[6] W. Page Keeton et al., Prosser and Keeton on the Law of Torts (5th ed. 1984).

- The organization did not take all economically feasible steps to provide a reasonable level of security.

STANDARDS OF LIABILITY

Recent court cases and legislation have used some new terms to define standards of liability and burdens of proof:

Strict liability. The act requires no proof of intent to commit the act.

Vicarious liability. In general, corporations are vicariously liable for the actionable conduct of their employees performed in the scope of their employment. This traditional doctrine applies to aiding and abetting a crime or a conspiracy to commit a crime, wherein an employee acts with the knowledge and intention of facilitating the commission of a crime.

Derivative liability. Acts and intent of corporate officers and agents are imputable to the corporate entity.

Responsible corporate officer doctrine. This applies to any corporate officer or employee "standing in responsible relation" to a forbidden act. Liability can arise if the officer could have prevented or corrected a violation and failed to do so. This is strict liability, focussing on the act only; no mental element is involved.

This is a critical doctrine with significant implications. An officer has a positive duty to seek out and remedy violations when they occur, and a duty to implement measures that will ensure that violations will not occur. The responsible corporate officer doctrine derives from the Food, Drug, and Cosmetic Act (see *U.S. v. Park*) and the Clean Water Act. While normally applied to services and products that affect the health and well-being of the public, the doctrine could easily cover mental well-being, such as privacy. The doctrine forces the corporate officer to define which risks he or she should know because the officer is likely to be held to an affirmative duty of care concerning those risks.

Willful blindness or indifference. The defendant intentionally avoids knowing a situation or act that will incriminate. Willfulness is a disregard for the governing statute and an indifference to its requirements.

Flagrant organizational indifference. The organization consciously avoids learning about and observing the requirements of a statute.

"Ostrich" instruction. This permits a jury to infer guilty knowledge from a combination of suspicion and indifference to the truth. (See *U.S. v. Giovannetti.*)

Rogue employee. One who, for his or her own benefit, commits an illegal act or whose conduct violates company policy and procedure and despite in-place efforts to prevent such an act.

Collective or aggregate knowledge. Where the knowledge possessed by several employees adds up to willful knowledge or yields a guilty state of mind, required by the statute, the organization can be liable for violating the statute.

OTHER SOURCES OF POTENTIAL LIABILITY

Statutes, administrative rulings, and common law cases have expanded executives' and corporations' responsibilities and liabilities, especially in the workplace.

State statutes also regulate corporate behavior and can have requirements similar to federal statutes. In some instances, federal law may preempt state statutes. One comprehensive statute, and perhaps a model for other states, is California's Corporate Criminal Liability Act. This law has a number of consumer protection features and stiff individual and corporate sanctions and fines.

DEFAMATION

Wrongful or negligent disclosure of private or embarrassing facts usually requires such information be communicated to more than one person. Any disclosure of false information could lead to a defamation suit. Defamation has two types of communication: defamation via print, writing, pictures, or signs is called libel; and slander, which is defamation by speech. Both are communication of false information to a third party that injures a person's or a business's reputation—causing bad opinion, public hatred, ridicule, or disgrace.

Other elements of defamation include: the reasonable identification of the defamed person and damage to reputation. If the defamation refers to a public figure or is a matter of public concern, it must be proved that the defamatory language was false, and that it was communicated knowingly or with a reckless disregard as to the truth or falsity of the information.

The basic defenses to defamation are the facts of the statement being probably true and a privilege can be invoked. Privilege can be absolute, which is reserved for government officials, such as judges and legislators, and the content of most public records. The press has a qualified or limited privilege to report on matters of public interest that might go unreported. This qualified privilege can be lost if the information is in error and malice can be shown.

A HYPOTHETICAL CASE OF WHAT NOT TO DO

An employer suspects an employee is stealing and fires him. As a warning to other employees, the employer sticks a notice on the company bulletin board stating that the employee has been fired for stealing company property. Could the employer be liable in defamation per se? You bet. What if the notice had been posted on the company's E-mail system? It's the same as the bulletin board.

The above is based on an actual case. The employee was never tried or convicted of theft, there was no proof a theft ever took place. His ex-employer was found liable of damaging the employee's reputation, proof of which was the former employee's many rejections for employment.

EEOC GUIDELINES ON WORKPLACE HARASSMENT

The Equal Employment Opportunity Commission (EEOC) has issued guidelines on harassment, which may include the following conduct relating to race, religion, gender, national origin, age, or disability:

- Epithets
- Slurs
- Negative stereotyping
- Threats
- Hostile acts
- Denigrating or hostile written or graphic material posted or circulated in the workplace

The EEOC notes that an employer is liable for its employees' conduct and the conduct of its agents and supervisory employees whenever the employer knows or should know of harassment by its employees or agents and fails to take immediate and appropriate corrective action. Further employers who fail to implement an explicit policy against harassment that is clearly and regularly communicated to employees, and employers who fail to establish an accessible procedure allowing employees to make harassment complaints known to appropriate officials are also liable.

WICKED WORDS

Generally, bad or abusive words are of three types: profane, obscene, or insulting. In law, these words can create a conflict between an individual's First Amendment right of free speech and restrictions statutes or employers impose. Cases are nearly always situation-specific, however, the courts have offered some guidance. The Supreme Court in *Chaplinsky v. New Hampshire* stated:

> There are certain well-defined and narrowly limited classes of speech; the prevention and punishment of which have never been thought to raise any constitutional problem. These include the lewd and obscene, the profane, the libelous, and the insulting or "fighting" words—those which by their very utterance inflict injury or tend to incite an immediate breach of the peace . . . Such utterances are no essential part of any exposition of ideas, and are of such slight social value as a step to truth that any benefit that may be derived from them is clearly outweighed by the social interest in order and morality.

In *R.A.V. v. City of Saint Paul,* Justice Scalia used sexual harassment as a proscribable class of speech:

> Thus, for example, sexually derogatory "fighting words" among other words, may produce a violation of Title VII's general prohibition against sexual discrimination in employment practices. Where the government does not target conduct on the basis of its expressive content, acts are not shielded from regulation merely because they express a discriminatory idea or philosophy.

THE TORT OF OUTRAGE

An employee who is the target of abusive verbal or E-mail messages, such as racial slurs or epithets, could bring a tort of outrage

claim against the employer. This tort comes from "one who by extreme and outrageous conduct intentionally or recklessly causes severe emotional distress to another is subject to liability for such emotional distress . . ."

"Intentional infliction of emotional distress" could also come from threats of violence. Note that is not necessary to show that someone who threatens another with physical harm is likely to commit acts of violence. There is simply no certain correlation between threats and violent acts. While a person might fit a "violence-prone profile," profiles generalize personality traits denominated from a large group; their use in assessing individual risks is limited. However, knowing that an employee uses threatening and violence-laden language should alert an employer to a general duty to foresee the possibility of violence.

USING BIAS-FREE LANGUAGE

Managers and employees should learn to expurgate demeaning, dehumanizing, and patronizing words from their communications, especially E-mail, and use words that are free from bias and stereotypes. In each of the above cases, it is easy to see how acts and words can be directed via a company's communications system.

Aim for clarity and accuracy. It is better to refer to people with disabilities, rather than the disabled. For example, refer to a person with a specific disability, as blind, deaf, or epileptic, or walks with a cane or uses crutches.

Where possible, avoid using the male pronoun when you want to refer to both men and women—either eliminate it, replace it with a neutral article (the or its), recast the sentence in a passive voice, or rewrite the sentence to eliminate unnecessary pronouns. Rewriting often does the best job since it forces a discipline towards precision.

DIRECTORS AND OFFICERS LIABILITY

The basic legal duties of corporate directors are loyalty and care. First, avoid conflicts of interest, and second, be informed about company operations, do not make poorly considered decisions or be negligent.

APPENDIX C

The corporate director and officer relationship to stockholders is similar to that of an agent to a principal. Liability is similar in that it may be based upon failure to perform a statutory or a common law duty. Failure to use ordinary care and prudence, when it results in loss, can generate liability.

APPENDIX D
SUGGESTED READINGS

Androphy, J. *White Collar Crime*. Colorado Springs, CO: Shepard's/McGraw-Hill, 1992.

Baker, D. and Brandel, R. *Law of Electronic Funds Transfer Systems*. New York: Warren, Gorham & Lamont, 1988.

Bender, David. *Computer Law: Evidence and Procedure*. New York: Matthew Bender, 1978.

Bernacchi, Richard L. *A Guide to the Legal and Management Aspects of Computer Technology*. Boston: Little, Brown and Co., 1986.

Block, Dennis J. and Pickholz, Marvin J. *The Internal Corporate Investigation*. New York: Practicing Law Institute, 1980.

Bologna, Jack. *Computer Crime: Wave of the Future*. Madison, WI: Assets Protection, 1981.

———*Handbook on Corporate Fraud*. Stoneham, MA: Butterworths, Inc., 1993.

Bologna, Jack and Shaw, Paul. *Fraud Awareness Manual*. Madison, WI: Assets Protection, 1995.

Brickey, Kathleen. *Corporate Criminal Liability*. Deerfield, IL: Callaghan & Co., 1989.

Brinson, Dianne J. and Radcliffe, Mark F. *Multimedia Law and Business Handbook*. Menlo Park, CA: Ladera Press, 1996.

Brown, L. *The Legal Audit: Corporate Internal Investigation*. New York: Clark Boardman Co., 1990.

Business Conference Board. *Corporate Ethics*. New York: The Conference Board, 1990.

Comer, Michael. *Corporate Fraud*. New York: McGraw-Hill, 1977.

Committee of Sponsoring Organizations of the Treadway Commission (COSO). *Internal Control—Integrated Framework.* New York: The Committee of Sponsoring Organizations of the Treadway Commission, 1992.

Disaster Recovery Yellow Pages. Newton, MA: The Systems Audit Group, 1999.

Dorr, Robert C. and Munch, Christopher H. *Protecting Trade Secrets, Patents, Copyrights, and Trademarks.* 2nd ed. New York: John Wiley & Sons, Inc., 1995.

Fischer, L. Richard. *The Law of Financial Privacy.* 2nd ed. New York: Warren, Gorham & Lamont, 1991.

Forensic Services Directory. Princeton, NJ: National Forensic Center, (annual).

Frank, P., ed. *Litigation Services Handbook.* New York: John Wiley & Sons, 1990.

Goldblatt, M. *Preventive Law in Corporate Practice.* New York: Matthew Bender, 1991.

Hannon, L. *Legal Side of Private Security.* Westport, CT: Greenwood Publishing Group, 1992.

Hartsfield, H. *Investigating Employee Conduct.* Deerfield, IL: Callaghan & Co., 1988.

Kramer, M.W. *Investigative Techniques in Complex Financial Crimes.* Washington, DC: National Institute on Economic Crime, 1989.

Lee, Lewis C. and Davidson, J. Scott. *Intellectual Property for the Internet.* New York: John Wiley and Sons, Inc., 1997.

Longley, D., Shain, M., and Caelli, W. *Information Security Dictionary of Concepts, Standards and Terms.* New York: Stockton Press, 1993.

Milgrim, Roger M. *Milgrim on Trade Secrets.* Albany, NY: Matthew Bender, 1994.

Nimmer, Raymond T. *The Law of Computer Technology.* Revised edition. New York: Warren, Gorham & Lamont, 1994.

Obermaier, H. *White Collar Crime.* New York: Law & Seminars Press, 1990.

Parker, Donn B. *Fighting Computer Crime.* New York: John Wiley and Sons, Inc., 1998.

Perritt, Henry H., Jr. *Law and the Information Superhighway*. New York: John Wiley & Sons, Inc., 1996.

Schwartz, M. *Guidelines for Bias-Free Writing*. Bloomington, IN: Indiana University Press, 1995.

Shaw, Paul. *Managing Legal and Security Risks in Computing and Communications*. Woburn, MA: Butterworth Heinemann, 1998.

Skupsky, D. *Legal Requirements for Microfilm, Computer, and Optical Disk Records*. Denver, CO: Information Requirements Clearinghouse, 1994.

———*Recordkeeping Requirements*. Denver, CO: Information Requirements Clearinghouse, 1989.

Sigler, J. and Murphy, J. *Corporate Lawbreaking and Interactive Compliance*. Westport, CT: Greenwood Publishing Group, 1991.

Soble, Ronald L. and Dallos, Robert E. *The Impossible Dream: The Equity Funding Story, the Fraud of the Century*. New York: Putnam, 1975.

Soma, John T. *Computer Technology and the Law*. Colorado Springs, CO: Shepard's/McGraw-Hill, 1983 and 1995 Supplement.

Renesse, Rudolf Van. *Optical Document Security*. New York: John Wiley & Sons, Inc., 1995.

Vaughan, D. *Controlling Unlawful Organizational Behavior—Social Structure and Corporate Misconduct*. Chicago: University of Chicago Press, 1983.

Vergani, James V. and Shue, Virginia V. *Fundamentals of Computer-High Technology Law*. Philadelphia: American Law Institute/American Bar Association, 1991.

Villa, J. *Banking Crimes: Fraud, Money Laundering, and Embezzlement*. New York: Clark Boardman, 1988.

Wagner, Charles. *The CPA and Computer Fraud*. Lexington, MA: Lexington Books, 1979.

Wasik, M. *Crime and the Computer*. Cary, NC: Oxford University Press, 1991.

Wood, Charles W. *Information Security Policies Made Easy*. Sausalito, CA: Baseline Software, 1994.

Wright, Benjamin. *The Law of Electronic Commerce: EDI, E-mail, and the Internet*. 2nd ed. Boston: Little, Brown & Company, 1995.

INDEX